Ten Studies in Christian Stewardship
Based on Luther's Small Catechism

# STEWARDS APPOINTED

by
RAYMOND M. OLSON

Augsburg Publishing House, Minneapolis

# STEWARDS APPOINTED

Ten Studies in Christian Stewardship
based on Luther's Small Catechism

© 1958 Augsburg Publishing House

Library of Congress Catalog Card No. 58-10319

Manufactured in the United States of America

# Preface

These chapters have been prepared with a mixture of reluctance and desire.

The desire has been present because of a personal compulsion to search many sides of the Christian faith for those truths which are woven into "Christian stewardship"; to share those truths with others in the Christian family; to spotlight some of the implications of stewardship for the Christian teacher who seeks to lead children and youth into the rewards of Christian living.

The reluctance has been present because Christian stewardship is not subject to ready definition, certainly not until a good part of a lifetime has been spent in searching its meaning in the light of Holy Scripture. These chapters cannot treat the subject thoroughly. There are great gaps which only more years and more experience can fill. The insights of many other Christian stewards should have been brought into such a study.

Nevertheless, the desire has been more insistent than the reluctance and these chapters have taken form. May this small light on a great truth bring new light to others, increasing the understanding of Christian stewardship throughout the Church and the Churches.

RAYMOND M. OLSON
*Director of Stewardship*
The Evangelical Lutheran Church
Minneapolis, Minnesota

# Contents

# TEACHER TRAINING COURSE BOOKS

Published under the auspices of the Board of Christian
Education of The Evangelical Lutheran Church

Ten Studies in Biblical History by Jacob Tanner

Ten Studies in the Creed by Jacob Tanner

Ten Studies in Church Doctrines by Jacob Tanner

Ten Studies in Personal Evangelism by O. Gornitzka

Ten Studies in Prayer by Emil Erpestad

Ten Studies on the Church Through the Centuries by Melva Rorem
(A revision of C. A. Wendell's "Little Journeys in His Kingdom")

Ten Studies on God's Plan in Prophecy by R. A. Ofstedal

Ten Studies on the Holy Spirit by J. N. Kildahl

Ten Studies on the Lutheran Church by G. M. Bruce

Ten Studies on the Sacraments by Alf M. Kraabel

The Child in Your Midst by Raymond Olson
(Ten Studies in Understanding Children)

The Law Perfect by Gerhard E. Frost
(Ten Studies on the Commandments)

Winning the Nations by Andrew S. Burgess
(Ten Studies in Foreign Missions)

We Learn to Teach by Hortense Storvick
(Ten Studies in Parish Education)

Stewards Appointed by Raymond M. Olson
(Ten Studies in Christian Stewardship based on Luther's Small Catechism)

---

Luther's Large Catechism

*A "guide question" to keep in mind
as you read this chapter:*

**What is the difference between a "Christian
steward" and a really "responsible person"?**

## FOR GROUP DISCUSSION

Can a Christian be a poor steward?

Are non-Christians sometimes good stewards?

Why should a "good steward" of life, property, or abilities become a Christian?

What is the relationship of being a good steward, and depending on salvation by works?

# Chapter One

# The Meaning of a Word

A word is a basket in which we may carry an idea from one person to another. A word is the summing up of truth and experience on the part of a man or a race. With a word a man hopes to transfer that truth and that experience to other men and to other races. Words are a necessary part of communication in our world. We are isolated from one another, unless we can lay claim to these vehicles for transporting ideas and letting them move back and forth among us intelligibly, vigorously and purposefully.

Words often acquire special and technical meaning in certain life situations. The farmer becomes accustomed to a certain vocabulary in connection with his occupation. The doctor uses a specialized vocabulary in the world in which he moves. The lawyer is dependent upon specialized words with specialized meanings. This is true in every profession, in every trade, in every walk of life and in every category of society. A specialized vocabulary is also characteristic of the Christian church and the Christian religion.

One of the problems in using specialized words is that the uninitiated and uninformed conclude there is something mysterious and difficult to understand behind an unfamiliar word or phrase. This happens in the area of our religious faith, as much as it does in any other area of life. One of the special words of the Chris-

3

tian church and the Christian revelation is the word
translated from Greek to English as "stewardship." It
has sometimes been suggested that we ought to drop the
word out of our religious vocabulary, because it has
gathered certain limited and untrue meanings along
the way. It cannot and will not be so easily set aside,
however. It is a word that is in our Bible. It ought not
be exchanged for some other words or word. We must
rather seek to understand its meaning as we find it in
the Scripture and then properly translate it into our
Christian faith and Christian life. It is the purpose of
this book to devote itself to that end.

This word "stewardship" has come to have some commonly accepted definitions. These definitions are not
necessarily the kind found in books, but the kind which
flow most naturally out of the interpretations we make
to each other through the use of the word. If we were
to have the members of a group write out their understanding of its meaning, it is very probable that most
of the definitions would in some way say that stewardship deals with the giving of money to the church. This
might mean the giving of money to the local congregation, to a church body, or to some church organization.
On the part of some people it might be expanded to
mean giving to any kind of organization or agency, but
normally they would have in mind one which is Christian or at least religious in its character and purpose.

This commonly accepted meaning for the word is giv-
en emphasis by the fact that in many American Protes-
tant churches there is some office or department which
is officially designated with the title of "stewardship."
In nearly all cases, such offices have responsibilities which
are largely financial in character and which especially
involve the encouragement of congregations in providing

financial support for the mission, educational and charitable work of the Church.

## STEWARDSHIP INCLUDES MANY THINGS

While the commonly accepted meaning of the word is the one indicated above, there is also wide recognition, within the Christian church, that there are other areas of life where the Christian man is to exercise a "stewardship" given him by God. The Parable of the Talents is often used to illustrate the fact that each person has been given certain unique personal skills, inherited talents, and particular abilities. It is a part of his responsibility to accept these with mingled humility and self-respect, keeping them sharp and useful for the service of God and of the world which God loves, improving them constantly.

A part of stewardship is the responsibility for the use of time. The Christian is to make the best possible use of his time for God and man, whether in his vocation, his avocation, or his recreation. He is to appropriate it victoriously and creatively to achieve what God wants accomplished in this world.

Another area for Christian stewardship is the management and use of the world's natural resources. Each person is to plan the careful use of these resources so they will be used wisely without waste, and with concern for generations yet to come. Conservation and development of these blessings are the practice of unselfish Christian living in a visible way.

There is also a stewardship of the body. The Christian will see in his body the earthly residence of his eternal soul. He will recognize his responsibility to live within acceptable rules of health as a part of his stewardship of this particular gift of God to him.

Most clearly the Christian steward is a steward of the Gospel. This is the greatest treasure with which he is entrusted. It must be his concern so to use all he is and has that the Christian message will be kept clear and will be sent forth freely and actively among men. It will be his purpose to cultivate the desire of others to share generously in such a concern. This is a part of the accounting due to his Lord in the stewardship which he holds.

There are other facets of stewardship which are commonly recognized and could be identified here, but the areas of concern given will illustrate the fact that the word is not limited to money, and certainly not to the money which is given to the Christian cause.

## NEVERTHELESS MONEY IS INVOLVED

The fact that stewardship is commonly understood to mean the giving of money does not indicate that this is a completely wrong idea. There is a valid relationship between the way a Christian uses his money and his call to support the Christian cause. This is one of the ways in which he gives expression to Christian faith and life. Unless some part of what a man has is given for the great purposes which center in the Gospel, it is manifest that something is fundamentally wrong with his entire relationship to his Lord and Savior. This consecration of possession to the service of Christ and His Church must continue to have the full attention of Christian people. The Church most certainly believes there is a stewardship of money, and a stewardship which involves the giving of money. Money provides power. It can damage or build. It always brings spiritual consequences through its use. The Bible makes very clear that God examines what we do with all we have and all we get. It makes clear that God has a claim on part of our money to achieve directly His purposes in us and in this world.

The critical nature of the stewardship of money and other material possessions is revealed in the handling and distributing of the total amount we have, apart from gifts to Christian causes. This is true whether these possessions be personal or whether they are those over which the individual simply exercises authority and control. The Christian steward cannot avoid responsibility for his total use of money and goods throughout each year of his life.

Such an understanding of money and property underscores certain aspects of Christian decision. We cannot give attention to this part of life without making decisions and being accountable to God for them. One of these decisions is the admission that no material good is actually our own, but belongs to God and is to be yielded to His service. This is unavoidable requirement for the man who commits himself and his life to Jesus Christ.

The use of our money is a particularly critical point for self-examination. We are tested as to what we really think about the Christian message. When we give joyously and in faith our own spiritual life is deepened. This, in turn, strengthens the Church and contributes to the spiritual well-being of the Christian community in which we move.

## STEWARDSHIP IS FELLOWSHIP

No stewardship is fulfilled in isolation. The family of God in the world is a large family. Each member of it must recognize he is dependent upon others if his life is to attain any measure of its God-given possibilities. So intimately are we bound together that we cannot avoid thinking of our stewardship as a corporate responsibility. We are called to work together, to watch over the welfare of the earth together, to nurture the life of the Church together. Stewardship is fellowship of the highest order. The greatest possible purpose of life draws us together with others who have seen the same vision, who have been crowned with the same high office.

The noble institutions of civilization, therefore, become the vehicles through which we may join with others in the fulfilling of the plan of God for our lives. Government beckons us to pour our corporate best into seeking the welfare of society. We are companions in our efforts to be responsible citizens. Education calls us to claim its possibilities for the development and true enrichment of men. Widely varied responsibilities lie ready, with posts for all. Health and welfare agencies, ministering to the distresses of men, invite all manner of God's stewards to their avenues of service. When approached by one person alone, the tasks are beyond consideration, but when approached with group concern, major accomplishments are possible.

The Christian Church, the noblest institution of them all, bears witness to the possibilities of a stewardship accomplished in fellowship with others. The tasks of the Church are immense, but they can be faced when we face them together, with the mutual encouragements which will sustain us all.

## A DEFINITION

It is clear that this word stewardship has no single and limited meaning. We can find some of the most thoughtful studies of the word and its meaning by turning to definitions and explanations which are current in Christian groups.

Probably the definition which is most commonly used at present is that credited to the Department of Steward-ship and Benevolence of the National Council of Church-es. It reads:

"Christian Stewardship is the practice of systematic and proportionate giving of time, abilities and material possessions based on the conviction that these are a trust from God, to be used in His service for the benefit of all mankind in grateful acknowledgment of Christ's redeeming love."

There are many elements to commend this definition to the thoughtful and sympathetic study of the Chris-tian Church. It brings together in a brief statement some of the most specific applications of truths related to this word and to this Christian concept.

Dr. T. A. Kantonen, in his excellent book *A Theology For Christian Stewardship* writes:

"When the concept of stewardship is developed in its total New Testament context it implies even more than trusteeship and responsibility. It contains the idea of partnership. The relation between master and servant gives way to the relation between friends working together for the realization of a common purpose. . . . Christian stewardship is a family affair. Not merely to work for God as his agents and administrators of his property, but to work with him as his children, sharing his purposes, his resources, his very nature—such is the high status of Christian stewards." (p. 4-5)

Dr. J. E. Herrman, Stewardship Counselor of The Lutheran Church - Missouri Synod, in his book *The Chief Steward* writes this:

"The stewardship life is a life completely dedicated to God through faith in Christ Jesus. Martin Luther said, 'If anyone should rap at the door of my heart and ask, "Who lives here?"'

I would answer, "Martin Luther once lived here, but Martin Luther has moved out, and Jesus Christ has moved in!" ' Paul's first words after his conversion were, 'Lord, what wilt Thou have me do?' He gave his whole life to God. David Livingston expressed the complete dedication of his life to the King in these immortal words: 'I will place no value on anything I have or may possess in relation to the Kingdom of Christ. If anything I have will advance the interests of that Kingdom, it shall be given away or kept only as by giving or keeping it I may promote the glory of Him to whom I owe all my hope and faith in time and eternity.' " (p. 13)

Paul's letter to the Ephesians describes the Christian steward and his stewardship more clearly than any other single book of the Bible. While he does not provide a formal definition of the word, the truths which he expresses are the truths of stewardship in the Christian Church. Three passages are especially to be noted:

1:12 "We who first hoped in Christ have been destined and appointed to live for the praise of his glory."

1:4-5 "He chose us in him before the foundation of the world, that we should be holy and blameless before him. He destined us in love to be his sons through Jesus Christ."

2:10 "For we are his workmanship, created in Christ Jesus for good works, which God prepared beforehand, that we should walk in them."

## BIBLICAL AND THEOLOGICAL STUDY

The Christian truth and concept involved in the word stewardship has such far-reaching implications and such depths to it that it needs the careful study and attention of each generation of Christian people. We ought not to assume that we can simply take the word from our Fathers, without living fully into its meaning and its lessons for us. It is particularly important that those who are called to the task of teaching in the Christian Church shall have good foundation at this point. There is a need of biblical study and theological examination of the word and of the idea of stewardship. The fact that fresh attention is now being given to it among the churches of the world makes it even more important that we shall have a part of such a continuing study.

Once again, it is worth noting the especially unique and helpful contribution which Dr. T. A. Kantonen has made. In the first chapter of his book he calls attention to the word in Greek and the meaning given to it in translation:

"Stewardship is the English word used to translate the New Testament word *oikonomia*. The Greek word is a compound of *oikos*, meaning house, and *nomos*, meaning law. It refers thus to the management of a house or of household affairs. In classical Greek it had a variety of connotations but principally that of financial administration, the meaning retained in its direct derivatives such as economy and economics. In the Gospels an *oikonomos*, steward, is a slave or hired servant to whom the owner entrusts the management of his household. "Who then is the faithful and wise steward, whom his master will set over his household, to give them their portion of food at the proper time?" The term acquires a spiritual significance, however, when our Lord uses it as a metaphor to describe a man's management of his whole life in responsibility to God. In the Pauline epistles *oikonomia* becomes a definite religious concept. Paul uses it in defining his commission as a preacher of the gospel. He speaks of himself as steward of the grace of God and of the mysteries of God. He even resorts to this term to define Christ's administration of God's redemptive plan for the world. Stewardship obtains its highest meaning and its strongest theological foundation when the apostle relates it to God's purpose "which he set forth in Christ as a plan (literally stewardship plan, *oikonomia*) for the fulness of time, to unite all things in him, things in heaven and things on earth." (p. 2-3)

Our need for continual study of this Christian truth is particularly pressing because of the current emphasis upon "the giving of money" as synonymous with "stewardship." While money is a part of stewardship and while money is to be given for the Christian cause, this is but a part of the stewardship life and must be kept in proper perspective.

We probably cannot return to the basic scriptural ground without a thoroughgoing searching of the Scripture throughout our churches. It is particularly important that all who teach and learn in our churches should make this a part of their study.

Furthermore, we need such study lest people be driven away from the whole truth through an over-emphasis upon one aspect of it. There are great riches of Christian living which ought to be found and enjoyed. They can be lost if we emphasize only one aspect of Christian stewardship. There is call for exploration in order to find the complete meaning as God expresses it for us in Scripture and reveals it for our blessing and our spiritual maturing.

We are living in a time when the Christian churches of the world are finding increased occasion for conversations together, sharing their insights into biblical truths. If there is to be a common ground on which all of the churches in their various national settings can comprehend together the central meaning of stewardship, we will all do well to join in a thorough-going examination of what it means. Thus, as God leads us, we will be moved into the unique contributions which each church can properly make out its own life and its own need.

The exploration of the Christian steward's relationship to God and man is a lifelong exploration. We will never fully grasp what it means, what we are to do with our lives and what we are to do with the world in which we live. We will not live long enough, nor will the sanc-

tifying process take place effectively enough for us ever
to know all the dimensions of Christian stewardship.
At the same time, the breadth and depth and height
of this truth beckons every Christian person to understand it and to live in it.

## LUTHER'S SMALL CATECHISM

It is the intention of this little volume to study some
of the implications of Christian stewardship in the Christian faith as it is set forth in Luther's small Catechism.
The chapters which follow will make this exploration.
They will seek to restore a greater perspective for the
Christian truth which is carried in the phrase: "Christian Stewardship."

## A DEFINITION AND DESCRIPTION

With no great desire to replace other definitions, but
under a compulsion to put into some form the convictions which underlie these chapters, the following definition and description of stewardship is presented:

Christian stewardship is the response of the Christian to
God's love and purpose, the recognition that he is appointed
by God to use his life responsibly, productively and thankfully.
This is his stewardship because Christ died for him. It is
possible because Christ has risen.

God clearly intends that the Christian shall develop and
use his capacities, his abilities and his precious years. Placed
in a material world, he is to share in managing and using it
so as to serve God and the human family for which it was
created.

All the best fruits of the centuries have been entrusted to
the Christian, as a member of this family, including worthy
institutions of religion, government, education and scientific
research. He is called to use this material, moral and spiritual

inheritance for the enrichment of his own generation and generations not yet born.

Above all, the Christian is a steward of the Gospel—the sacred revelation of the will of God for man through Jesus Christ. He is called to devote regularly generous portions of his time, money and all other available resources for the present and future proclamation of this Gospel, and to join eagerly with others in carrying out this supreme mission.

The King's Library

*A "guide question" to keep in mind
as you read this chapter:*

**Do our traditional concepts of the first three
commandments need overhauling?**

## FOR GROUP DISCUSSION

What are the idols of our generation—in our community?

What is the relation of the first commandment and the
third article of our faith as explained by Martin
Luther?

As Christian stewards, entrusted with God's name, should
we not use His name *more?* When?

Does not being a good steward of property and of family
projects call for some kinds of real work to be done on
Sunday?

# Chapter Two

# The Steward Confronts
# the Great First Commandment

The Ten Commandments provide the opening section of Luther's Small Catechism, our guide in this examination of the word "stewardship." The Commandments are the record of God's moral law revealed to man so that he might not lose sight of his true nature, and might not forget the kind of life to which he is called.

When Jesus spoke of the Commandments, he divided them into two parts. He reminded us that the first three Commandments speak of love to God and the last seven speak of love to our neighbor.

"You shall love the Lord your God with all your heart and with all your soul and with all your mind. This is the great and first commandment, and the second is like it. You shall love your neighbor as yourself." (Matt. 22:37-39)

In these Commandments, Jesus reveals areas for great moral and spiritual decision. He summarizes them in unmistakable and simple language. Here He gives guidance concerning the right way for His people to live. Here is His revelation of the moral absolutes which are built into human life. These absolutes will inevitably reveal the tragic fact of sin and rebellion, even in those people who have responded to His redeeming grace. The whole testimony of human history is in accord with the

17

experience of every person that this law of God cannot be kept perfectly. It constantly stands in judgment on man. At the same time, it invites men to accept and claim the forgiving love of God revealed in the redeeming Christ. The person who is thus "in Christ" and at peace with God then dares to return to these Commandments. In them he finds his instruction for a good and righteous life. In them he finds the promise of the gracious work which Christ will perform in his life through the Holy Spirit.

Call this man now by the name of "Christian Steward." Having entered into God's love and forgiveness, he is to be helped to understand his stewardship and to enter upon it with thankful devotion. He is to be shown the nature of the astounding trust which God has given him and the pattern of life he is called to follow.

He accepts these Commandments thankfully, even though he is shaken by their reminder of his moral weakness. They give him important signs along his way through life—signs to guide him lest he defeat God's intentions for him. They become for him a way of identifying the work of the Holy Spirit in his life. He finds evidence in these Commandments of the guiding love of God, a love which shows man how to live, and which continually forgives and restores a repentant and consecrated steward.

### THE FIRST COMMANDMENT

"I am the Lord thy God. Thou shalt have no other gods before me."

*What is meant by this?* We should fear, love, and trust in God above all things.

The First Commandment makes very clear that man belongs to God. There are many things we do not under-

stand about ourselves. We may be perplexed about the
purpose of our life and the full nature of our destiny.
There is no perplexity on God's part however as He
speaks here.

"What then shall we say to this? If God is for us, who is
against us?" (Romans 8:31)

"Can a woman forget her suckling child, that she should
have no compassion on the son of her womb? Even these
may forget, yet I will not forget you. Behold, I have graven
you on the palms of my hands; your walls are continually
before me." (Isaiah 49:15-16)

We are not our own. Nor are we primarily the property of our family, or our society, or our nation. We
are thoroughly and completely committed from the
moment life begins. We owe everything we are to God.
Nothing we will get out of life will be without His prior
claim resting upon it and upon us. While He is under
no obligation to us, we are under unremitting obligation
to Him. We have not been given freedom to rule our
lives and the world in which we find ourselves apart
from the purposes and intentions of God. It is highly
important since God has planned it this way, that we
understand the plan. Otherwise, we should make short
and dismal use of what we might assume to be freedom
to use life without responsibility.

The steward is to be under no illusions about his
position. He is steward and not Master. He is sinner
and not Savior. He is to be guided. He is not the Guide.
He is the property manager, not the property owner.
He is the one entrusted, not the one who gives the trust.
The purposes of life are revealed to him; he is not the
determiner of those purposes. In his true devotion to
God, he will find no sound reason to question this ar-
rangement, but will understand that it is established

in this way by the perfect love and infinite wisdom of God.

One of the great temptations of the steward is to become preoccupied with the things which have been created, with the wonders and riches of the world in which he lives, with things that come under his own influence and control. This preoccupation with the created wealth, the beauty and goodness of the earth easily leads to the development of attitudes, loyalties and primary interests which bring separation from the Master. When God warns against this possibility, He is standing guard over us and over all those who might be hurt by our failure to remember who we are.

Each generation produces its idols, those things to which it gives its highest attention and final loyalty. We have them in our time. Our children will find others developing in their time. We are drawn to such idols because they serve our purposes. They fit our appetites and desires. They do not embarrass us. They satisfy us.

The person who has been called to serve the true God is in danger of having substitutions for God creep into his life and experience. One of the current points of temptation is that he wants "a religion that works." This is the spirit of our age. He seeks a religious experience which caters to his needs as he understands them. In so doing, he settles for a god made according to his own pattern, a god made to please and fit his own ideas of religion. The true God is lost in the process and this "servant of God" gets thoroughly adrift.

The person called to be God's steward in life must keep special watch over his spiritual loyalties. He must remember he is in constant danger of creating sorrow and evil, when he is intended to produce goodness and joy. To march off on his own, without living continually and humbly within his stewardship, is to miss the mark and to lose touch with God. Not only will he miss his own true destiny, but the whole of mankind will be afflicted in that failure. Something of the good purpose of God in the life of a man will have failed to materialize and the whole earth will be the poorer. Not only does this good thing fail to come forth out of such a man's life, but the evil in him grows more vicious when his gods are no greater than his own ideas and desires. Not only can we become persons who fail to contribute for good in the world, but we can become, increasingly, the kind of people who actively contribute to evil. We are called to be stewards and builders for God; but we can pervert our trust to thorough-going destructiveness.

Money, wealth and property have consistently remained among man's most popular idols, gaining his loyal attention, interest and preoccupation. But money, wealth and property have been created by God, have come into being as a part of the world which He brought forth. They have been a part of the gift of God to His people. They have been intended for use in accomplishing the perfectly good and desirable purposes of God. Money and wealth and property can be of inestimable good when used with the recognition that they belong to God. They can be limitless evil when used as though they belong to men. When used as our own with accountability to no one, money and property are destructive forces. When they are used to serve our purposes without reference to God's purposes, they become, sooner or later, a corroding element in the world.

The Christian steward meets one of his major temptations at the point of money and property. This test of his steward's relationship is heavy and critical. It is for

this reason that any consideration of Christian stewardship must involve the use of money. The issues become
particularly and sharply drawn here, where it is determined whether a man's loyalty and obligation are
to God, or whether a man's intention is only to possess
material things for himself for use according to his own
will, desire and appetite.

The First Commandment is *a call* to the Christian
steward to guard against all such idolatries. It is a call
to acknowledge continually that the one true God alone
has a claim upon him, and to remember that this claim
is a good and beneficent one. This Commandment is
*a witness* that he should faithfully and daily offer to
God what he is and has, bringing his selfishness under
the discipline of using the material world to do God's
work. It is *a reminder* to the Christian steward that he
should seek to grow in the knowledge of the God who is
revealed, with no side journeys to create gods of his own
liking. It is *an invitation* to seek from Jesus Christ, God's
Son, the cleansing, restoration and abiding grace which
will make of a man what this Commandment calls him
to be.

## THE SECOND COMMANDMENT

"Thou shalt not take the name of the Lord thy God in vain;
for the Lord will not hold him guiltless that taketh His name
in vain."

*What is meant by this?* We should fear and love God so
that we do not curse, swear, conjure, lie, or deceive by His
name, but call upon Him in every time of need, and worship
Him with prayer, praise, and thanksgiving.

The reading of the Second Commandment is a reminder of the word of Jesus that we are called to a
complete and unreserved love for God. This Command-

ment is another of the gifts of God to humanity so that
a response of love from man might be as free and natural
as possible. The Second Commandment is clearly intended to draw away all of the debris of history and
all of the insolence of a man's heart in order to keep
in clear relief the person and the name of God.

The man who is called to be a Christian steward is
entrusted with the name of God. Great issues are involved in keeping this name an honored and respected
one in the earth. This is no trivial trust, but one to
which a man may well devote his fullest and finest capacities.

It is important, for the sake of the steward himself,
that the name of God is not taken in vain. It is important
in his whole relationship to God that every part of
God's revelation concerning Himself shall be continually remembered and reverently considered. If he uses
God's name without respect, it is a proof that something
serious has happened in his own attitude toward the one
whose steward he is. Any attitude of irreverence and
disrespect emphasizes the lack of importance this man
gives to God. When such a state of mind and such attitudes are present, it means that all of the real foundations for *stewardship* are gone. It means that this person
is adrift in a world without compass and chart, without
purpose and hope.

On the other hand, to give honor and strength and
glory to God's name, is to give Him the proper place of
attention and reverence. If He is the all-important one
to us, there will be no doubt of our willingness to count
on Him in all our responsibilities or needs.

The matter of being entrusted with God's name is
not only important for the steward himself. It is also
important for all of his brothers who will be affected by

what he himself thinks of God and says about him.
His sense of respect and reverence for God's name is
revealed in the use he makes of his life. His respect for
God's name defines the values which he holds in the
service of God. Only as God's name is pre-eminent in
the mind and heart of each Christian steward is it possible for each life to be given unreservedly to God's purposes revealed most specifically in the Christian gospel.
This name must not lose its glory. It must not lose its
identification. It must not suffer corrosion. This is a
large part of our trust.

The name of God is to be so used that it will call
forth from every man who comes to know God, prayer,
praise and thanksgiving. It is through His name with
all of its biblical meaning that we have our knowledge
of who He is and what He intends.

The Second Commandment also tells us that since
Christian stewards are entrusted with the name of God,
they must also be dedicated to truth. Gardiner Day says
this:

> "It was the Commandment that guarded the integrity of
> a man's word and all society rested and still rests upon this
> fundamental honesty of individual with individual. If a man
> takes an oath in the name of God and does not keep it,
> the foundation of all human relations is cracked." (Gardiner
> M. Day, *Old Wine In New Bottles*, Morehouse-Gorham Co.)

Luther in his explanation closely allies this Commandment with the matter of taking an oath in the name of
God. To take such an oath, underscores the sacredness
of truth. To bring disrespect and dishonor to God and
disintegration of society's respect for His name is to
destroy thoroughly the foundation for truth itself.

The Christian steward who considers that truth is a
sacred trust must himself be a trustworthy person. Only

God can make him this. God *will* make him this only
as he himself respects the nature of God.

Luther also reminds us that Christian stewards should
call upon the name of God every day. They should do
this because they fear and love God. They know they
would not dare face life without Him. They have come
to know out of their daily experience of His mercy that
He is a loving and merciful God. They should call upon
Him because this is the natural outflow of their experience and their need, and because they understand that
God desires such communication with them. Their prayer
and praise is the natural evidence of a living relationship
with Him.

The Christian steward offers his prayer as a part of
his acknowledgement of need. He discovers that he cannot accomplish very much by himself. He is daily reminded of his sin and his failure. He is perplexed in
knowing how to be a faithful steward in the service of
God. Therefore, he lives in abiding fellowship with
God, with constant reference to the One who has called
him and appointed him.

This use of God's name, by praying to Him, is also
a part of our worship of God. Such worship underscores
the Commandment and serves to draw man and God
closer and closer together. This is adoration of Him.
It is giving Him honor and homage.

## THE THIRD COMMANDMENT

"Remember the Sabbath day, to keep it holy."

*What is meant by this?* We should fear and love God so
that we do not despise His word and the preaching of the
same, but deem it holy, and gladly hear and learn it.

This is the Third of the Commandments which call
us to live life in an unreserved and unqualified love

for God. Such a response from man does not take place unless he is continually refreshed in his acquaintance with all that God is and all that God does. This continual acquaintance is essential to the fruitful work of the Holy Spirit in us.

The command to "Remember the Sabbath day" is an important part of the counsel of God to man. It is a very necessary sign along our way to show us how to live. To ignore it is to bring trouble and tragedy to us and to our children. It is necessary for our own sakes to live in accord with this Commandment of God. It is necessary for the proper fulfilling of our calling to have this week by week tryst with our Creator, Redeemer and Sanctifier.

This Third Commandment, with its direct attention to the Sabbath day, reveals vividly many of the needs in which the Christian steward is included along with all of his mortal companions.

Look at some of the things which God accomplishes by having His people observe the Sabbath Day. The observance of this day produces a regular occasion for remembering the supreme fact that we are God's people. Out of our involvement in many other matters in a busy world, we are called to attention concerning who we are. Our primary loyalties and commitments are made fresh again. We review the fact that we belong to Him on the basis of creation, that we have been established in Him by the redeeming cross of His Son and have been kept by the continuing work of the Holy Spirit. The Christian steward cannot possibly permit himself to carry on in his appointment without this weekly reminder of who he is and what has been done for him.

This God-given day of rest is also a time for remem-

bering that it was on the seventh day that God rested
and considered his created world to be very good. There
are many experiences on the part of mankind which
produce disillusionment and discouragement. It is not
unusual to lose sight of what God considered this world
to be, and to lose sight of what God has in mind for
His creation. The day which is God's special day in
the week becomes a time for getting our bearings again.
It is a time for assurance and hope. It is the moment
to be renewed in the consecration of our lives to the
good purposes of God.

The Sabbath day is a time for worship. As we considered the Second Commandment, we noted how thoroughly important worship is for the Christian steward.
His worship of God is a part of his recommitment of
himself to God. It is the time when he lays hold upon
all his resources to bear witness to God's glory and goodness. The Sabbath Day provides him with the specific
time and circumstance in which this worship may reach
its regular climax. The day is a gift to him to keep him
a worshiping person and to draw him out of his ab-
sorption with himself and his world.

This day in the week, as we meet together with the
other members of the congregation, becomes a time for
remembering that we are not on the journey of life alone.
It is a time for realizing that we are among many fine
and wonderful—and needy—brethren. We remember in
these hours together on Sunday that God has other people, that we need one another, in the experience of re-
pentance, in the experience of forgiving grace, and our
life commission. The Christian steward ought to find
encouragement in such hours from the witness and devotion of his brothers. He ought to find indications of

how much the total use of his life and his resources is
needed in the Christian family, and also in the non-
Christian world in which that family exists.

Certainly it is unquestioned that the Sabbath day
is a time for remembering the importance of the Word
of God. It is the day for giving special attention to the
reading of the Scripture, the proclaiming of its gospel,
and the searching of all of its meaning for our present
life and the life to come. The Christian church lives
by feeding on this Word of God. It cannot live by feeding on its own philosophies and own experiences. It
must return to this central place, this bread of life. The
very presence of the Word of God in the midst of the
Sabbath day is a necessary experience for the Christian
steward. His spiritual need is met in and through it.

This Sabbath day is a time for remembering the great
commission. Jesus Christ, our Lord and Savior, has called
all of His people to go and make disciples of all nations. There are many excuses which arise and barriers
which are placed to the fulfilling of this commission.
They are found within the hearts of Christian stewards,
as well as in circumstances of the life of the church and
the society in which the church finds itself. Nevertheless,
the Christian church, and each Christian steward, must
seek the moments and the circumstances where the reminder of the commission will be made strong and firm
again. This is a primary part of the good purpose of
God for us. We dare not permit it to be set aside. We
need the Sabbath day for this purpose.

The Third Commandment, with all of the benefits
which it brings for the spiritual life of man, must also
be understood as a way by which God expresses His concern for the physical life of man. This one day in seven
is a time for restoration of the body through rest. God

understands very well the weariness which can come to His creatures. He commanded from the beginning that we should take time for renewal of our body. Our stewardship is exercised through our body.

In Luther's explanation to this article, we noted that "we should fear and love God so that we do not despise His Word and the preaching of the same." In this Commandment, as in the others, our response is not the response of slaves, but the response of Christian stewards as the redeemed people of God. It is because we fear and love God that we remember the Sabbath day. It is because we know that this is for our good and for our blessing. It is because we seek for the sacred moments in His presence that we obey the Commandment. We rejoice in the assurance that Jesus Christ, our Lord, works in us the desire to keep this Holy Day. In obeying this commandment we know we are bearing witness to our Master and we are refreshing and renewing our own lives.

*A "guide question" to keep in mind
as you read this chapter:*

**What is the Christian steward's relationship
to property values and to human values?**

## FOR GROUP DISCUSSION

Why do you think so many church people align themselves with political movements that emphasize property
values rather than with liberal movements emphasizing
human values?

How can Christian stewards help, rather than hinder, one
another in fulfilling these commandments?

Do Christian stewards generally apply these commandments equally to all people — migrant workers, for in-
stance? — or negroes? — or one's employees? — or one's
employer? — or one's competitors?

# Chapter Three

# The Steward Confronts the Great Second Commandment

The consideration of the last seven Commandments is, of course, inseparably entwined with the meaning of the first three. It is our love for God which produces our love for our neighbor. It is the relationship which we have with God which produces the proper kind of relationship in our society in general and with individual persons in particular. It is important to recall the word of Jesus—"and the second is like it, you shall love your neighbor as yourself."

It is this concept of love for our neighbor which provides the setting and the spirit in which our stewardship is fulfilled. It is this spiritual condition of our being which enfolds and then responds to other people who are also the objects of the love of God. It is the realization of our common place in His divine affection which guides us in the way we are to live among others.

## THE FOURTH COMMANDMENT

"Honor thy father and thy mother, that thy days may be long upon the land which the Lord thy God giveth thee."

*What is meant by this?* We should fear and love God so that we do not despise our parents and superiors, nor provoke them to anger, but honor, serve, obey, love and esteem them.

The Fourth Commandment has been understood by the church as the basis of instruction concerning the basic social institutions of the family, the state and the church. Christian stewards, as people who have been appointed to serve God in the world, are reminded at this point to give reverence, honor and dignity of position to their father and mother, to all other ancestors and benefactors.

This reverence, honor and appreciation of worth begins with recognizing that God has given the foregoing generations a very significant place in our own lives and in the circumstances in which we find ourselves. Our recognition of our dependence on previous generations for what we have of learning, culture, and religious heritage, produces an awareness of our debt to them. All that we have, all that we are and a very high proportion of that which we will eventually be or do can be traced directly to "our parents and superiors."

We are called as Christian stewards to have proper respect and to give honor to our parents and all others in authority. This calling involves the principle that all integrity and social worth begins at home. If we contribute to any 'disrespect for our own home, we contribute to disrespect for all homes, and to their disintegration in society. Even though there may be certain things about a person's home which he considers below standard, this is not a valid reason for him to refuse honor to his parents. Even though his family's standards may have their faults, nevertheless, those standards likely curb some of man's most dangerous impulses and desires, and can stand guard in moments of severe temptation. We invite great trouble for ourselves, and in turn for total society, when we break away from the standards, the principles, the ideals of father and mother. The

Christian steward will recognize the valid discipline which this Commandment orders for his own life and for the proper structure of society.

If we are to understand this Commandment, we must recognize that Christian stewards are entrusted with an inheritance out of the past. This comes to us from our parents, from the state and from the church. And this is clearly God's plan. We do not start fresh with each new generation. We receive from the generations their accumulated wisdom and accomplishments; then we are called to carry on in the period of our own stewardship.

No generation can make a new beginning. We would destroy ourselves if we attempted to do so.

There are always people, of course, who do not understand and appreciate the inheritance which is entrusted to them. Just as sons and daughters can take an inheritance of money and squander it, so there are persons who squander the inheritance which is given to them by all others who have preceded them. They become "marauding persons." They are "the saboteurs of civilization." This possibility of being a squanderer is one which confronts every one of us. It is possible for a person to become so completely separated from the purposes of God for him, that he makes waste of his life and everything else he has been given. There is a heart-disturbing tragedy continually paraded before us—that men can take life, and the resources of the world, and the resources of civilization, and be irresponsible vandals with it all. The fact that it can be so should drive Christian stewards in all soberness to ask God to make them something other.

When God in this Commandment tells us to "honor," we understand that He is telling us to keep faith with our father and mother and with all the rest who have contributed to the cultural wealth which comes into our hands. To keep faith with them is to receive that cultural heritage as a trust, and to recognize our responsibility to use it as persons of spiritual integrity. This is a part of what it means to be a steward of God. We stand in the stream of the generations, receiving gifts from the past into our hands and our control. Certainly we are under obligation to pass everything on undiminished. We are held responsible for seeing that no decay sets in among things entrusted to us. Not only are we called to transfer to others without loss, but we are called to remember Jesus' parable about the man who buried his talent in the earth. We should be soberly responsible for taking the treasure of our social and religious inheritance and then passing it on with new riches and new quality added to it.

In the stream of the generations, it is not least important that men and women who have received the heritage of the organized church and its institutions will appreciate this particular part of their trust. We who have so received are to take these results of the prayers, efforts and devotion of others and to see to it that our educational and charitable institutions shall be stronger as the result of the support and devotion which we have given to them. It is not enough simply to see that current bills are paid by congregations, and minimum amounts given to the institutions of the church. We are called to do far more than this as those who "honor father and mother." As Christian stewards called to a responsible, productive and satisfying use of life, we are under obligation from God to transmit a good inheritance. This particularly says to us that we must consider

those whose biological or spiritual ancestors we will be.
T. S. Eliot said—"When I speak of the family, I have
in mind a bond which embraces a longer period of time
than the present age; a piety toward the dead however
obscure and a solicitude for the unborn, however re-
mote." (T. S. Eliot, *Notes Toward The Definition of
Culture,* Harcourt, Brace and Co., Inc.)

## THE FIFTH COMMANDMENT

"Thou shalt not kill."

*What is meant by this?* We should fear and love God so
that we do our neighbor no bodily harm nor cause him any
suffering, but help and befriend him in every need.

This is another Commandment which deals with man
as a social being, a member of the human family. We
approach it remembering the word of Jesus that fulfilling all these last seven Commandments is done in the
spirit of love for our neighbor flowing out of our love
for God.

The Christian steward, assigned as he is to serve the
purposes of God, gets an additional insight into his responsibility through this command "Thou shalt not
kill." Here he is entrusted with maintaining in word
and action the value God has placed upon life. He is
to maintain this value within his own attitudes and to
act accordingly in all areas of human activity. This value
which God has placed upon life is understood most
clearly when we recognize that man has been created in
God's image. This means that he is the best of God's
creation. Since he holds this pre-eminent place in creation, it follows very naturally that the person who is
in this world in the service of God should be greatly

concerned about the value of man's life in contrast with the rest of creation. We may understand very well that we are responsible for the growing things of the earth and the treasures under the earth. We may understand without much difficulty that the wealth which comes out of the resources of the land is a part of the stewardship of man. But this Commandment is God's way of reminding us that we have a stewardship which goes beyond the material, and into the realm of the very life of human kind.

Even though our experience in life makes it clear that there is much evil in man and much which is not to be emulated, nevertheless it is perfectly apparent that God loves man unendingly, even when he is in rebellion. If that is God's attitude to humanity, even with His knowing what is wrong with us, then this is also surely to be our attitude as His servants living in the world.

One of the reasons for this high value on human life is that God has placed in every person remarkable possibilities for the mortal years he has, as well as for the immortal centuries which are to come. The treasures in the human spirit are of far greater value, and have far greater possibilities than treasures located elsewhere in God's created world. When we accept our God-given trust, it is inevitable that we find a large part of it involved with the safeguarding and enriching of human life. Life needs safeguarding. It needs this for security and for the opportunity to develop. God, through this Commandment, is protecting life against willful destruction and is in the process, reminding us why it ought to be so.

It is apparent from this command of God that the Christian steward must not only recognize the value of the life of his neighbor, but he must exercise himself for the welfare of his neighbor. This is a challenge to our very basic attitudes. By nature we are inclined to get rid of our problem with our neighbor by getting rid of our neighbor. This is the most direct way of solving the problem. At least it seems so to man until he discovers that he thus creates far greater problems for himself and society.

If the Christian wills to exercise himself for the good of another man, he can learn from his Master what he should do. He is called to a glad and complete yielding of self in the service of others. He is to act out the love of God living and moving in his heart.

The Fifth Commandment calls us to help and befriend our neighbor in every bodily need. This means an intelligent, active, constructive activity on behalf of the sick, the neglected, the hungry, the weak, the shut-in, the fallen and wayward, the prisoner, and the long list of men and women with substantial personal problems.

Furthermore, the Christian steward is called to take an active interest in gaining the best possible living conditions for all people. It becomes his duty and privilege to take an active interest in the civic affairs of his community and country. He is to be found on the side of justice and all efforts which will produce equity for people. The whole matter of social conditions must have his attention, for it is in the social situation that life can be safeguarded or can be maimed and destroyed. His devotion to the creation of good living conditions should extend into political affairs and economic policy and practice. He is expected to be concerned about the opportunity which his neighbor has to earn his daily bread. We are called to be concerned about the total security of the life of our neighbor. His life is lived in a world where the conditions of existence have a profound effect upon him. To be a steward of God, appointed to represent Him in the affairs of men, is to give ourselves to all this.

## THE SIXTH COMMANDMENT

"Thou shalt not commit adultery."

*What is meant by this?* We should fear and love God so that we lead a chaste and pure life in word and deed, and that husband and wife love and honor each other.

This command of God tells the Christian steward that he is entrusted with maintaining the value God has placed upon man's sexuality and on marriage. When the entire message of the Bible is taken as one message, it is clear that God is declaring that sex is a good gift of His. It is a sacred and not a sordid gift. Therefore, it should be gratefully accepted and devoutly regarded. God tells us our sexuality must never be degraded by wrong use.

It is also a part of God's trust that marriage should be an expression of love. To love another person is to want for him what God wants for him. Love does not seek its own satisfaction, but it seeks what is best for the partner. A Christian steward should understand this about his own marriage, and then devote himself to encouraging such love in all marriages.

The spirit of this Commandment is a call to the steward of God to keep his body in temperance, soberness and chastity. This can only happen when we are free from bondage to our appetites. Such freedom from bondage calls for earnest self-discipline. It also calls for continued reliance upon our Lord, and for prayer for His watchfulness over us in our temptations.

If a man does not keep his body under control as this Commandment indicates he should, then he will be defiling what God has made holy. This is not only defiling of the body, but the defiling of a relationship between man and woman which is intended to be the most noble of human relationships. If desires rule, then we make nothing more than beasts of ourselves, and the other party becomes simply a thing to satisfy desire. In the process of breaking the Commandment, we break two people who ought to be God's people. Then we produce a kind of festering infection in society which reaches far beyond us.

In this Commandment it is clear that the Christian steward must do something for the good of others. (There is always a positive and constructive side to these Commandments.) This contribution for the good of others will be made both in anticipation of marriage and also in the marriage relationship. Furthermore, it will be made in relationship to all persons with whom there might be a temptation to commit adultery. It should be added that it ought to be exercised also in relation to society, not least the Christian community. It is plain to anyone who will look, that in the wrecking of one home the adulterer weakens all homes.

We are called to efforts which will contribute to firm, happy, God-pleasing marriages, and to the cultivation of a social and religious condition which will produce marriages where the partners can become spiritually mature and can live to the enriching of each other's lives. God intends that we should demonstrate to each new gener-

ation the God-pleasing basis which they should seek for
marriage, and the spirit in which they should enter it.

### THE SEVENTH COMMANDMENT

"Thou shalt not steal."

*What is meant by this?* We should fear and love God so
that we do not rob our neighbor of his money or property,
nor bring them into our possession by unfair dealing or fraud,
but help him to improve and protect his property and living.

The Seventh Commandment tells us that the Christian steward, appointed by God to do His will and work
in the world, is expected to stand by God's interpretation of property and its proper use. This point of view
begins with an understanding that the earth and its
riches were created before man was. These riches of the
field and the forest, the mine and the sea, are so abound-
ing that there is enough for the material needs of all
people. According to the Scripture, man was placed in
the midst of this great wealth, these magnificent resources "to have dominion." In other words, God made
man his responsible steward of all these riches. We are
under the responsibility and we are given the joy of
managing it all for the best welfare of man and for
achieving God's will thereby. This entire relationship
which man has to the earth and its resources is the
basic ground on which this Commandment must be understood.

Our acquisition of money and property is to be according to God's will. This means that we acquire it
through work. Work has great benefits for the human
race and must not be undervalued. Of course, there
are many ways to get money and property without work.

We see continually how this is done through stealing, robbing and cheating, using false weights and measures, underpaying workers, doing a job poorly, selling goods to satisfy evil appetites and through gambling.

It should be particularly noted that the return which we get for our labor is based upon the integrity of both the worker and the employer. This whole relationship is one which comes continually under the scrutiny of God who has set us in this world to use our lives fully and constructively. The way we acquire our income and possessions is a demonstration of the degree of social and religious responsibility which we have.

Not only our acquisition of property, but our use of it is to be according to the will of God. The Bible is quite clear about what this means. Scripture's concern for the use of material things is one which must give us pause, not only when these things are our own, but also when they belong to others and we are involved for a time in the management of them.

The use of these things is best understood when we recognize that responsibility goes along with possession —responsibility to our ancestors, from whom we have received so much, and responsibility to succeeding generations. We have absolutely no right to use property for ourselves alone apart from an awareness of our place in the whole history of people!

In an organized society the use of money and property includes taxation. The payment of taxes, through which governmental functions are carried out, is a part of responsible stewardship. For the Christian man, taxes are not to be placed in some non-spiritual category. They have many Christian implications for him. He is under obligation to pay them as a necessary part of government and social order. He may question their nature and amount. Indeed as a citizen he has that right and that responsibility. But the Christian's responsible use of money includes the mature acceptance of the principle of taxation. Our use of material wealth should promote the material and spiritual welfare of our world, not only our own welfare, but also that of the people who live in the world with us. The proper use of wealth builds the user's Christian character. Improper use of it will destroy the same.

This Seventh Commandment is intimately related to all Scriptural declarations that wise and God-pleasing use of property includes giving it, investing it, to fulfill the divine commission of God. This was what God taught from the beginning in setting up a plan for the giving of tithes and offerings by His people. Certainly they were not a wealthy people. To a very great extent, they were wanderers on the earth. But they were commanded by God to give these tithes and offerings. He wanted them to understand that this was involved in the very earning of their income and the ingathering of the fruit of the land. He had a claim upon it right from the beginning.

Both Scripture and human experience tell that such giving should express the gratitude and love of the giver. It is to produce spiritual growth in the giver. For this reason, Christian giving, not to be thought of as a tax or a financial leverage on church members, is seen as the expression of an inner life. It is thought of as evidence of the love of God flowing through the life of a Christian steward.

The wise steward will give with thoughtfulness and careful purpose to serve constructive spiritual and social ends. He should not allow himself to give carelessly and irresponsibly. He should take into account the most strategic ways in which he can serve the church and meet the substantial benevolent needs of his community and nation. Such careful consideration will cause him to weigh the importance of joining his gifts with those of other responsible people. It is not wise to plan our giving without reference to the plans of others. We give our best accounting when we act as careful stewards in company with other thoughtful people.

Careful use of our possessions comes to its last consideration when we plan the final disposal of the estate we accumulate. It is not responsible stewardship to leave the settling of our estate to chance. That settling ought to have the same kind of careful and prayerful attention that we give to all the other uses of property entrusted to us by God. As those appointed by God to serve His plan for the world, our plans for disposing of our estate at our death will most certainly be made in the light of the needs of our family, our church and our society as best we understand them. This is part of our acceptance of the place we hold in the stream of the generations.

The Seventh Commandment sets before us very plainly the positive relationship we are to have to wealth in this world. We are *entrusted* with it both in the acquiring and in the using of it. To fall to the level of gambling or stealing in order to get it is to destroy our own integrity and our own relationship with the Master who has entrusted this material world to our care. To take from others is to injure them and to become a sad cancer in society. God calls us through this Commandment to be concerned for our own good *and* for the good of our neighbors. We are His representatives in the whole matter of getting and using property.

## THE EIGHTH COMMANDMENT

"Thou shalt not bear false witness against thy neighbor."

*What is meant by this?* We should fear and love God so that we do not deceitfully belie, betray, backbite, nor slander our neighbor, but apologize for him, speak well of him, and put the most charitable construction on all that he does.

A good name is such a valuable asset for a man that God has used one of His Commandments to safeguard it. The Christian steward is entrusted with the welfare of his neighbor and of society by guarding the good name of others.

Standing guard over the reputation of other people calls for positive action. We are expected to defend our neighbor's reputation out of genuine love for him. We are expected to put the best interpretation on all that he says and does. There will always be voices seeking to destroy the name and reputation of a man. The Christian steward will recognize that he must have no part in this, but that he is committed to an entirely different evaluation and action.

He will be very much aware of the evil that comes from gossip and malicious speculation. He will understand that speaking evil about people is the expression of evil in the heart of the speaker. It is the revelation of a degradation which is a far cry from the concern of God for a man.

There are serious implications for us as we look to our courts and their dispensing of justice in the exercise of legal processes. Law and order are essential to the well-being of people in a society. They are necessary for our security in living our lives most satisfactorily. The Eighth Commandment calls before us the evil which results when witnesses in courts of law perjure themselves; when lawyers, juries and judges are dishonest; or when they conduct themselves in such a way as to bring disrespect for law. Any weakening of truthful speaking in court quickly encourages lawlessness and brings danger to a secure social existence. When God gave this Commandment He was telling us that we must watch over the name and reputation of each other, both in court and out of it. If we fail to do this persistently and out of genuine concern for each other, we will reap a tragic harvest indeed.

The Christian steward is given this Commandment as a guide, for he is to speak good about others consistently. He knows that then he is living in accord with God's will and God's purpose. His habit of speaking good about his neighbor is an expression of the good that is in him as it has been produced and renewed under the stirring of the Spirit of God.

## THE NINTH AND TENTH COMMANDMENTS

"Thou shalt not covet thy neighbor's house."

*What is meant by this?* We should fear and love God so that we do not seek by craftiness to gain possession of our neighbor's inheritance or home, nor obtain them under pretense of a legal right, but assist and serve him in keeping the same.

"Thou shalt not covet thy neighbor's wife, nor his manservant, nor his maidservant, nor his cattle, nor anything that is thy neighbor's."

*What is meant by this?* We should fear and love God so that we do not estrange or entice away our neighbor's wife, servants, or cattle, but seek to have them remain and discharge their duty to him.

The two closing Commandments are the guiding word of God for a man in showing him the right way to live, and reflecting his responsibilities as a member of the human family. The Christian steward comes under examination here as he does in all of the preceding Commandments. Covetousness is seen as one of the major evils among men. When it is listed in the Bible, it is placed in the company of great evils, such as murder and adultery. Covetousness is the state of a man filled with an evil desire or lust for that which belongs to another. It is the willful nurture and indulgence of such a desire in thoughts and deeds. Covetousness is a sin against our neighbor. It reveals a wrong attitude toward him. It reveals that we are much more concerned about the things we can get from him than about the things we can do for him. To let the spirit of covetousness linger very long quickly destroys the love and constructive interest which God expects us to have in the life of our neighbor.

Furthermore, covetousness is a sin against God. It is bold ingratitude. We are stewards of what comes to us in God-pleasing ways. We go far beyond what God intended when we desire what God has not entrusted to us, but to another. The whole extent of our stewardship comes under scrutiny when we confront covetousness in our lives.

In this Commandment, too, it is clear that we are expected to conduct ourselves constructively and usefully. We are to earn our own living. By the effort we put forth we are to justify having what we have. It is wrong for us, according to God, to be reaching out around us for those things that we have not earned and to which we do not have a right.

It might also be added that in conducting ourselves

constructively among our brethren, we must earn the right for good men to have us around. We have no particular reason to assume that other people are under obligation to keep us in their company.

The antidote to covetousness is being with God and learning from Him. If the Christian steward will live in such a daily relationship with God, he will find contentment in what he has and in what God gives him to do. His great debt to God and to man is emphasized. This far-reaching obligation for what he already has will assume such proportion as to deny any kind of covetousness.

Daily association with God will fill us anew with His love, which then moves through us to other people. We stand our best chance of subduing the covetous spirit when it is overwhelmed through the change of heart which God alone can produce.

## IN SUMMARY

In this great Law of God the steward finds exceedingly clear guidance. This is God's plan for his life. Here are wide vistas of his stewardship. He knows that the full use of his life is intended to serve God and his neighbor. He learns to distrust his own desires and inclinations, submitting them rather to the absolutes of God. He experiences the challenge and the call to what his life could be if God should have His way with him. He is aware that these guideposts are for nobility, for those who are sons of the Kingdom of God. He dares to call on his Savior and Lord to direct him in such noble paths.

*A "guide question" to keep in mind
as you read this chapter:*

> Is "the fatherhood of God and the brother-
> hood of man" an adequate concept for the
> Christian steward?

## FOR GROUP DISCUSSION

What is the Christian steward's responsibility for outer
space?

In what ways are people of your own community "plunderers"?

Why do not Lutherans more often take the lead in government, industry, organized labor, science, art, education?

Should the church give more attention to man's understanding of government and current community problems?

# Chapter Four

# The Steward
# and His Divine Father

A Creed is a statement of belief. This can be a personal
statement. It can be the statement of a group of people
who hold a common faith. The Apostolic Creed is a
confession of faith of the Christian Church. It is not the
only Creed which the church has, but it is one commonly held throughout Christendom. The Apostolic
Creed incorporates the simple and essential elements of
what the Christian church believes and teaches about
God. Coming into existence early in the life of the
church, it has been confessed through the centuries by
millions of people.

This Creed, with its three articles, makes clear that
the Christian believes in a personal God. His is not a
belief about something or about someone, it is not a
belief primarily in theological conclusions. It is a faith
in a person. This fact of personal faith in another person is highly important for us to understand. We may
very well not know all there is to know about this God.
In truth, we will never come to such complete knowledge,
but it is still quite possible for us to thoroughly believe
in Him. We know Him to the extent that it is possible
for us to know Him, with faith moving beyond knowledge into the area of absolute trust.

Our faith in this God is that He will reveal what He

49

wants revealed about Himself, about His relationship
to our world and to us. It is our confidence that He will
do to us what He wants to do, and do through us what
He wants to have done. Our faith in this eternal Person
is one that is without reservation. It is one of complete
trust.

In this Creed, we confess our faith in a Triune God,
three persons in one. We believe this, even though we do
not understand such a mystery. It is not essential for us
that we shall fully understand. It is essential that we
unreservedly and completely commit ourselves to Him,
as He has revealed Himself.

Our stewardship gains much of its meaning from the
character of our relationship to this Triune God. We
do have a relationship to Him and a responsibility which
rises out of it. The exact nature of this relationship certainly does not come to any man fully developed and
explained. In fact, it is often understood only in very
small part. A person seems to discover over a period of
time and out of many lessons the many implications
of his relationship to this Triune God. The exploration
of this relationship is a lifelong exploration.

This relationship in which we exercise our stewardship
is one that ought to have fascination for every Christian
person. In it is the secret of how mortal man responds
to and serves the immortal God. Out of it comes the
sense of significant achievement in the use of our life.
This relationship is the most exciting fact of human
existence. Our lives belong to God. Placed in His created
world we are appointed to serve Him to the fullest. We
are called and chosen to be participants in those events
whereby God watches over and blesses His creation and
draws it unto Himself forever. The office of Christian

steward is no mean office. It has the overtones of eternity
in it.

## THE FIRST ARTICLE

"I believe in God the Father Almighty, Maker of heaven
and earth."

*What does this mean?* I believe that God has created me
and all that exists; that He has given and still preserves to
me my body and soul, my eyes and ears, and all my members,
my reason and all the powers of my soul, together with food
and raiment, home and family, and all my property; that He
daily provides abundantly for all the needs of my life; protects me from all danger, and guards and keeps me from
all evil; and that He does this purely out of fatherly and
divine goodness and mercy, without any merit or worthiness
in me; for all which I am in duty bound to thank, praise,
serve, and obey Him. This is most certainly true.

This First Article of the Apostolic Creed, summarizing
as it does the faith of the church in God the Father,
becomes a part of the exploration on the part of the
Christian steward. As he examines these words which
have been voiced by multitudes, he is confronted with
what the nature of his own faith ought to be and he is
introduced to many of the qualities of God as they are
revealed in the Scripture.

"I believe in God!" The Christian steward present
in this world with a divine appointment cannot settle
for an impersonal approach to the subject of God. He
is far too involved with who He is and what He wants
of man. When the Christian steward says he believes
in God, he is strongly emphasizing the fact that he does
not believe in himself. He does not find in himself the
ultimate. That must be somewhere else.

We believe in God because of His revelation to us. We are personally caught up in all we come to know about Him. When the Christian steward has made this his confession, he has found the supreme orientation for all of his work and for all of the years he will be given.

"I believe in God the Father Almighty." When we confess our faith in Him as our Heavenly Father, we are first of all saying that we believe He is the Father of Jesus Christ. He is the one who has done this amazing work of preparing a salvation for the world He created and sending His Son as the Incarnate Redeemer. This is the God in whom we say we believe. Furthermore, in this Article of our Faith, we confess that we believe He is the Father of all those who have been baptized into Christ and who believe the Gospel. This is the God to whom all the company of Christendom belongs. Therefore, He is not only the Master who assigns responsibility to a servant, nor an owner who gives directions to his steward, but He is the eternal and loving Father of that steward.

This is very important to the steward in understanding who he is and what his responsibilities are. There are many who are inclined to define Christian stewardship as being a matter of trustees and servants carrying out the will of God. This is only a part of the meaning of the relationship. The fact that He is our Father tells us that we are sons and heirs, not merely trustees. Christian stewardship is a family affair. We are watching over the Father's house. We are taking care of His affairs. This is a relationship of the most intimate kind. The stewardship of our life does not then become a burdensome duty, or a fretful obligation. It becomes the demonstration of a deep intimate relationship. In view of this relationship, our response can only be satisfied in the total response of yielding our life and all our resources to achieve the purposes of this family.

This Almighty Father has filled His created world with beauty and goodness. He has done it out of a love that is almost incomprehensible to the human spirit, for the world produces no love comparable to it. Luther, in his explanation of this article, makes us aware of this when he says—"And . . . He does this purely out of Fatherly and divine goodness and mercy, without merit or worthiness in me." Wherever we look around us in this world and in whatever we discover about its nature, we are continually confronted with the spirit of love and goodness which operated in its creation. If we are to be the stewards of such a Creator then we must be sympathetic to His purpose and use all of the resources of the earth in that same spirit. We must not permit ourselves or other men to be plunderers. We must be very sensitive to what God wants His material and spiritual world to be.

It is exceedingly important in the fulfilling of our stewardship to this God to remember His almighty and all-ruling character. This means that He had from the beginning a perfect design. He directed His creation to that end and He has continued to watch over it and guide it to that same end. The world is not out of control. Selfish and sinful man is not obstructing the final and ultimate purposes of God. We can be very sure that He will not be overruled by sin, nor by the fall of man. He intends to save the world. He intends to reconcile mankind with Himself and to redeem him. He will not give up and He does not want His people in their stewardship to give up either. This is a part of what it means to believe in the Father Almighty. We may have complete confidence as we give ourselves and our resources to His service.

"I believe in—the Maker of heaven and earth." Every bit of creation, all of heaven and earth and the universe around it, all the elements in the earth and upon it, all the operating forces which exist in creation, and all the magnificent qualities and capacities of man had their beginning in the mind and heart of God. This is what the Scripture says. This is what we believe as Christians and as stewards. This truth gives us proper orientation to the material world in which we find ourselves. This is not an evil, treacherous world. It is rather the creation of a God who saw it to be very good. This is a highly important fact to comprehend when we are called to be stewards of God. We can lay hold upon this material world, with all the forces that operate in it, and believe we are managing good things for good and holy purposes. We can be confident that wherever we turn we can move within the will and intention of the Heavenly Father, the Maker of heaven and earth.

There are those individuals who are under the conviction that there is a necessary separation between spiritual things and earthly things, and that the truly worthy preoccupation of man should be in the realm of spiritual things. This Article of our faith reassures us that both the spiritual and the earthly are under the rule of the same Creator. Therefore, as we receive from Him the blessing in both realms, we can with confidence exercise our stewardship in the whole.

The history of man is filled with the discoveries which man has made of God's creative imagination and generosity. Man has had reason for perpetual amazement at the lavishness of the gifts God placed in the created world for humankind. Man has explored the resources under the earth and the resources upon the earth with all its growing things. There seems to be no end to the variety, the beauty, the productiveness, the store-houses which God has provided. In each decade, even into this century, there have come new discoveries of new elements in new and unexpected places. The Maker of heaven and earth has indeed provided far beyond the imagination of any man.

Not only are there visible resources in the earth and upon it, but there are resources in the forces of nature which operate in the created world. These last decades have opened up entirely new conceptions of the structure of matter and sources of energy which can be harnessed for the benefit of humanity. We live in an atomic age. That very fact, bursting upon us with such speed, has made us even more aware that the resources which God may have stored up in this world are still far from un-derstood.

In addition to these resources, there are resources with-in man himself. Who is there who can fully understand the intellectual, emotional, spiritual, mystical and physi-cal treasures which are within the human being him-self. This is all a gift from the Creator's mind and heart. This is the way in which He has equipped us. Certainly it can be understood that the extent of the stewardship given to us by God is not yet known, and probably can not be in any single generation.

If this Almighty Father is the Maker of heaven and earth, then we need have no fear about its destiny. He is actively providing for it, guarding, protecting and keeping it. This fact gives us personal assurance as His selected stewards. We are not left in the midst of it all to be adrift from Him. We can be in active relationship. He is our ever present Father. As Luther says—"He daily provides abundantly for all the needs of my life, protects me from all danger and guards and keeps me from all evil." While this is true in His personal relationship to the individual, it is also true concerning His relationship to the entire world in which we live and in which we have our responsible assignment.

This part of our Christian faith, that we believe in God the Father Almighty—the Maker of heaven and earth, is bound to have additional personal significance for the Christian steward. Again, we are interested in the way Luther expresses it—"I believe that God has created me and all that exists; that He has given and still preserves to me my body and soul, my eyes, and ears, and all my members, my reason and all the powers of my soul, together with food and raiment, home and family, and all my property." This is a joyous confession. This is a reassuring statement. The God who watches over the far reaches of the universe is the God who has created me and preserves me, and meets my daily need.

The stewardship which is ours is not only religious activity in response to this God. It is an activity in all of the areas and avenues of life. God has created the whole world. He has planned for the development within that world of many aspects of human existence. It is His intention that in His created world man shall be concerned about the family, about government, industry, business, science, art and education. Interest in and activity in any of these areas is the proper response of the steward to the world in which God has placed him.

Luther describes this stewardship of all things as explaining the vocation of Man. All activity is holy when it is within the intent and purpose of God. Every beneficial occupation has its place in the kind of a world

which God has made. God's intention for our life meets
us in the specific task to which He calls us. In our world
all Christian men have a vocation. They are given a way
in which to use their lives. The Christian steward knows
or ought to know that his occupation is a divine calling.
God has provided it for him and he is in it to serve God
and to serve his neighbor. His life work is not a secular
thing. It is a divine thing. We give some proof of our
faith when we do what He gives us to do with joy and
gratitude. Our life work is an important part of our
stewardship. It is the center around which we normally
build the rest of that stewardship.

## THE STEWARD DISCOVERS HIS PLACE

When the Christian steward makes an exploration of
the Christian faith and finds in it all the delineations of
his stewardship, he then discovers at least a part of his
place and responsibility in this creation.

Kagawa, in Japan, expressed this discovery in this way:

I cannot invent
New things,
Like the airships
Which sail
On silver wings;
But today
A wonderful thought
In the dawn was given,
And the stripes on my robe,
Shining from wear,
Were suddenly fair,
Bright with a light
Falling from Heaven—
Gold, and silver, and bronze
Lights from the windows of Heaven,

And the thought
Was this:
That a secret plan
Is hid in my hand;
That my hand is big,
Big,
Because of this plan.

That God,
Who dwells in my hand,
Knows this secret plan
Of the things He will do for the world
Using my hand!

(Toyohiko Kagawa, "Songs of the Slums,"
Cokesbury Press.)

In this poetic form, Kagawa has described his re-
action to the discovery of the plan and purpose that
God has for his life. Luther in the explanation to
this First Article expresses the same thing when he says
—"For all which I am in duty bound to thank, praise,
serve, and obey Him." Both men are expressing something of that which they have discovered about their
stewardship.

One of the important discoveries of the steward as he
responds to this Father Almighty, Creator of heaven and
earth, is that this God is to be worshiped and adored
by the creature. It would be unthinkable for the Christian steward to get very far away from a recurring experience of worship. If he should begin to lose his sense
of adoration and wonder at the God who is revealed, he
would soon begin to lose the significance of his appointment and the implication of his relationship to this God.
Therefore, the steward will be one who adores his Crea-
ator.

A part of the discovery of the place we hold in this

creation is that the created world is placed under man's
control and use. God has given him his intelligence, his
emotions, his physical strength, to be dedicated to this
end. The original purpose of God, of course, was to have
man exercise dominion over all He had created in order
to bring it to greater flower and beauty in usefulness.
In the process, it must have been God's intention to
bring every possible benefit to man as he was exercising
his dominion in the midst of this creation.

It is also true about the place and responsibility of
the Christian steward that he himself is to be a creative
person. This is not to be understood in the same sense
as the creative God, but in the sense that God gives to
man unique and surprising abilities. These creative qualities which the steward has are to be used in humility,
subordinate to God's purpose and consistent with it.

After the fall of man and his rebellion against his
Creator, there was an added purpose which God had for
His world. This was the purpose of reconciliation, redemption and salvation. This is what we might call God's
missionary motive. This is the revelation of a God who
will not let His people go. The steward, placed in this
world by his Heavenly Father, has this added purpose
which must concern him and direct him all the time.
As it is the intention of God that the world shall be
saved, so it should be the intention of the steward that
the world shall be saved. The missionary motive which
directs the heart of God is the motive which must direct
the Christian steward in the exercises of his dominion
in the world.

In summary we can say that human existence is a
responsible existence. God has placed us here to make
something out of our lives and to make a substantial
contribution to humanity. At the same time, we can

say that human existence is a privileged existence. It is
an activity in the midst of God's creation which is carried out on the basis of the most intimate understanding
and relationship with the Almighty Father. This stewardship is to be accomplished in the spirit which Luther
described when he said we should "thank, praise, serve,
and obey Him."

*A "guide question" to keep in mind
as you read this chapter:*

**Why does freedom because of Christ also
seem to mean responsibility to Him?**

## FOR GROUP DISCUSSION

What does it mean to you that Jesus is *ascended?*

How does a person live under Christ in His Kingdom in
*this* community?

"Entrusted with the gospel"—what, specifically, does that
mean to you?

Can you find, in the Second Article, an answer to the
great question, "Who am I?"

# Chapter Five

# The Steward
# and His Redeemer

The Second Article of the Apostolic Creed is the Church's expression of faith in the person Jesus Christ. This is the Article which deals with the steward and his Redeemer. We believe in Christ as a person, not as an idea. We believe in Him, not in an abstract Christianity or an elusive "Christian way of life," but in a genuine person, true God and true man. This person is the one whom has made God known to us. That which we know of God is made valid and understandable because of Jesus Christ. Even while this is true, however, we quickly find the limits of our knowledge and understanding regarding Him. He is still God and we are still mortal men. It is beyond us to know Him completely.

There are important meanings for our stewardship in our relationship to this person, with all He is and all He intends for humankind. No one should attempt to interpret the meaning of Christian stewardship without having at the very center of that interpretation the person of Christ, the Son of God.

## THE SECOND ARTICLE

"And in Jesus Christ His only Son, our Lord; Who was conceived by the Holy Ghost, Born of the Virgin Mary; suffered under Pontius Pilate, Was crucified, dead and buried;

He descended into hell; The third day He arose again from the dead; He ascended into heaven, and sitteth on the right hand of God the Father Almighty; From Thence He shall come to judge the quick and the dead."

*What does this mean?* I believe that Jesus Christ, true God, begotten of the Father from eternity, and also true Man, born of the Virgin Mary, is my Lord; who has redeemed me, a lost and condemned creature, bought me and freed me from all sins, from death, and from the power of the devil; not with silver and gold, but with His holy and precious blood, and with His innocent sufferings and death; in order that I might be His own, live under Him in his kingdom, and serve Him in everlasting righteousness, innocence and blessedness; even as he is risen from the dead, and lives and reigns to all eternity. This is most certainly true.

The Christian steward, seeking to understand his stewardship, discovers that he is unavoidably involved with the person of Jesus Christ at two points. First of all, he is involved on the basis of his personal experience of the forgiveness of sins and the joy of redemption which comes because of who Christ is and what He has done. In the second place, he is involved because there are inevitable personal commitments and far-reaching responsibilities which arise from faith in this Christ.

Our stewardship is woven into our personal experience of the forgiveness of sin. From this there are very critical issues which arise for the person who is called to be a Christian steward. The full surrender of his life to Christ, which his stewardship implies, comes only when a man knows that Christ died for him—"for the love of Christ controls us because we are convinced that one has died for all; therefore, all have died and He died for all that those who live might live no longer for themselves, but for Him, who for their sake died and was raised." (II Cor. 5:14-15). The many aspects of Christian stewardship can be explained to a person at great length and he may understand intellectually what is involved. However, the actual yielding of his life and his resources will await the day when he has recognized that he is to live no longer for himself, but for the Christ who died for him and was raised again. The Christian Church cannot afford to bypass this central fact for the stewardship life. There are no short-cuts around it.

We are often inclined to conclude that stewardship is a description of what we have done or are going to do for God. We speak of it as a way of helping God. As a matter of truth, of course, what God does for us is the chief element in our stewardship. If it were not for what He has done and continues to do for us, there would be no point in talking about a concept of stewardship at all. We would not understand it, and we would be quite incapable of responding to it.

Our readiness to be stewards is dependent on our readiness to receive what this person Jesus Christ has to give us and what He has to do for us. Without Him, we cannot respond. Without Him, we are doomed to failure and destined to moral and spiritual wandering in the dark. There is no point in talking about the destiny and purpose of our lives until we have received from this divine person that supreme gift of forgiveness and everlasting life.

The relationship of the steward to Christ is understood in part in the words of Luther, who said,—"I believe that Jesus Christ, true God, begotten of the Father from eternity, and also true Man, born of the Virgin Mary, is my Lord."

In this expression of our faith, we recall that Jesus is a completely unique person. He is truly God and He is truly Man. Our relationship to Him is like no other relationship we have ever had or can ever have. Our stewardship, in the light of the person of Jesus, establishes us as being unique people ourselves, with a unique assignment in the midst of our world. We stand in relationship to a God who became incarnate and who walked among us.

We must never forget what a miracle was wrought that we might be restored to God, the miracle of the incarnation. When we confess the words "conceived by the Holy Ghost, born of the Virgin Mary," we are confessing that we believe in a God who would not forsake His world no matter how evil it had become. He came to us when we would never have come to Him. He callèd upon His stewards, who had forsaken their stewardship, to restore them again unto Himself. One can never lose sight of how God, in Christ, came down from Heaven to lift the world up out of its despair and ruin. The steward is brought up short when he confesses this part of the faith, because these words tell him something of the value which God has placed upon him.

This relationship of the steward to Christ is also understood in the words "suffered under Pontius Pilate, was crucified, dead, and buried." Luther comments on these words, in one of his most treasured passages: "Who has redeemed me, a lost and condemned creature, bought me and freed me from all sins, from death, and from the power of the devil; not with silver and gold, but with His holy and precious blood, and with His innocent sufferings and death."

While the steward has good reason to stand in wonder and thankfulness at the fact of the incarnation, he will discover the deepest meaning of it when he considers the suffering and crucifixion of our Lord. It is here he will remember there is nothing to which God will not stoop to draw us to Himself that He might give us life. In fact, as we consider this suffering, we know that without what Christ has done, there would be no life and there would be no hope. No revelation, no philosophy, no achievement of man has ever produced a basis by which man might believe he could have life without Jesus Christ.

The suffering and death of Jesus was necessary because of what had happened to man. Because it was necessary, it was done. The Christian steward must comprehend this to some degree, at least, if he is to find reason for the fulfilling of his stewardship appointment.

Why did Christ do this? Why did He die upon the Cross? The Cross is the means to the end He had in mind. It is not the end in itself. He came to seek and and to save that which was lost. He came to draw all men unto himself. This was the way necessary for Him to accomplish this.

The steward may find in Christ an example in self-giving. This may be a part of what the Cross tells him. But this is not the chief discovery. Christ was all alone in what He did there. No man can "take his cross" in the same sense that Christ took it. Our stewardship is not primarily to emulate Jesus Christ. Our stewardship is much more a recognition that through the Cross we have been redeemed unto God, that our lives belong to Him and are to be lived in a thankful and adoring response to this one who is truly our Savior and the Savior of the world.

The relationship of the steward to Christ is further understood in the words "He descended into hell; the third day He rose again from the dead; He ascended into Heaven, and sitteth on the right hand of God the Father Almighty; from thence He shall come to judge the quick and the dead." In Luther's explanation, he comments—"even as He is risen from the dead, and lives and reigns to all eternity."

To believe in Jesus Christ is to believe in a living contemporary. He is our living Lord. We believe in Him, not with the idea that He is only a part of the history of the past, but our believing in Him involves the present fact of His living and His rule over His Kingdom. In Luther's explanation of this Article, he said—"I believe that Jesus Christ—is my Lord." The word "is" should be underscored, for it was a very vital part of what Luther saw, even as it must be a vital part of what every Christian person and steward sees concerning Christ.

Since He is our living, present and contemporary Lord, we can have a living communion with Him. We are not sent as stewards to some foreign land, shut off from the one who has sent us. We are not called to the fulfilling of an assignment where we are entirely on our own. Our stewardship can be accomplished in a constant and daily fellowship with the one whose steward we are. The fact that He is a living and present Lord is to give special joy and courage and confidence to us in the use of our life.

In this Article we confess our faith in the fact of the ascension of Jesus. It is His ascension which makes it possible for Him to come to us. This is a very important part of the understanding of the stewardship relationship. We are not limited to our going to Him. If our faithful stewardship were to wait upon our readiness to go to Him, it would be far from being accomplished. In fact, it is this reluctance which often stands in our way. The fact of the ascension of Jesus, however, makes clear that He can and does come to us. He calls us, He reminds us of what we are to be. It should be added that His ascension makes it possible for us to pray to him. We are not trying to send our words back over the centuries. We are in conversation with the one who is risen from the dead, who has ascended into Heaven and is present at the right hand of God. We are not standing in isolation as we seek to be faithful in our trust. We can pour out our needs, our hopes, our joys, our desires, to Him in prayer.

It should also be noted that in this part of the confession we acknowledge that He will come to judge the quick and the dead. Since He is our judge, we will do well each day of our life to place the whole of our life before Him. There is nothing to be gained from hiding what we are and what we do. There is much to be gained from a constant exposure of all things to Christ, who is at the same time, our Savior and our Judge. He will help us see what we are meant to be and He will help us see what we have turned out to be. This experience the steward needs to have continually. He needs to have from Christ a continual refreshing of his mission. He needs daily renewal in the understanding of what he is meant to be and to do, and then, in order that he might in no way develop false pride and self-confidence, this Christ who is the judge, will in all compassion make clear to him what his failures and sins are.

We said earlier in this chapter that the Christian steward is involved with Jesus Christ at the point of his personal experience of the forgiveness of sins and the joy of redemption. We have seen in part how this personal experience in Christ is given identity in the words of the Second Article. We remind ourselves that our readiness and ability to be the true stewards of God is dependent upon receiving from Jesus Christ what He has to give us and what He wants to do for us. We are truly the stewards of God by His grace. We are equipped by Him for that which He has called us to be and to do. Stewards will inevitably, then, be thankful people who deeply love the God and Savior of their lives.

Earlier in the chapter it was stated that the steward is involved with Jesus Christ because of the personal commitments and responsibilities which rise from his faith in the Son of God. Luther summarized these in this way: "In order that I might be His own, live under Him in His Kingdom, and serve Him in everlasting righteousness, innocence and blessedness." This is as brief and clear a summary of the stewardship life as we can find in the documents of the Church.

"That I might be His own"—this is the pivotal and amazing fact for the steward. He is in a double sense a son and heir in God's kingdom. He is God's own by virtue of creation, but more particularly he is made God's own by the redeeming, reconciling work of Jesus Christ.

This fact of belonging to God is true because of what has been done. Its truth does not rest upon any satisfactory record of our stewardship which we may be able to produce. It is one of the primary responsibilities of the Christian steward to recognize that he is not his own, but belongs to Jesus Christ. In everything we plan to do with our life and in all of the uses we have for the resources around us, including our management of the heritage which comes out of the past, we act from the point of view that we belong to another. This belonging to Christ is not something that is a burden, but the recognition of a most glorious fact. The awareness of this relationship will govern all that we are and all that we do.

"Live under Him in His kingdom." The steward continually looks to his Savior. He lives under Him. This is a happy, thankful and fruitful relationship. The Christ is thus able to do for the steward and through the steward what He intends and desires. This is a most intimate relationship.

The kingdom, in which we live under Him, is in the present world. The kingdom is found wherever Jesus reigns. We find evidence of the kingdom in the individual life. We find it where Christian people are gathered together in the visible Christian Church. The aim of this kingdom is the restoration of all areas of life to the rule of Christ. The aim is the recovery of that which has gotten under the control of Satan and bringing it back to be under the control of a loving God. To live under Christ in His kingdom is to live within the Christian Church. It is to live within the Word of God, looking to it as a source of revelation and guidance for this life and the life to come. To live under Him in His kingdom is to use all of the means of grace. It includes a faithful use of the Holy Sacraments. These are His gifts to us for our spiritual strengthening. These are the channels through which His love and mercy are experienced by us. The steward is committed to live under Jesus Christ in His kingdom. It is for this that Christ became his Redeemer.

We are also aware that His kingdom is an eternal kingdom. The assurance of Christ's coming again is the assurance of a complete triumph of His kingdom. The Christian steward needs this assurance, and he finds it in this truth about the kingdom of God. Because Christ died for him and because he has entered into the life which Christ gives, he knows what is ahead. This is the strongest incentive the Christian steward can have as he carries on, seeking to serve his God in thankfulness and love. With the eternal kingdom ahead of him, there is strong reason for him to pour out his life and all that he has to serve the purposes of God. Furthermore, his missionary concern is increased. He knows that the world must become aware of Christ and His kingdom. This must not be treated as though it is incidental information. This is the truth which will determine whether men will live or die, whether they will be in the kingdom or outside the kingdom.

In seeing that the kingdom is eternal, the Christian steward has found the deepest perspective for his stewardship. The issues involved are not the issues for a day or a year or even for a lifetime. The issues involved are not how much a man should give to his church, or how much he should spend on himself, or how much time he should devote to his neighbor. All of these decisions and actions get their perspective from the fact that the steward lives under Christ in a kingdom which has eternal dimensions. When this is remembered, all other aspects of stewardship take their proper and subordinate place. Then the discussions of some of the responsibilities in the church become trivial indeed.

"Serve Him in everlasting righteousness, innocence and blessedness." Our Lord asks for consecrated action. He calls for single-minded, loyal and dependable service. We are committed to this service with the realization that it is the primary commitment of our life. In this comment of Luther, we are reminded that our service as Christian stewards is to be in continual righteousness. Our motives, our faith, our activity, will be searched by God. Furthermore, our service under God is to be the service of innocence. There is to be a single-mindedness in the use of our life and the use of our resources. We discover that this service is a blessed service. It is the right way to live. It is in accord with the plan of God. It is the way to enrich the lives of our neighbors. No matter how we approach it, this is right. The steward will reap the blessing.

This service of God which is our stewardship, includes being entrusted with the Christian gospel: "For our appeal does not spring from error or uncleanness, nor is it made with guile; but just as we have been approved by God to be entrusted with the gospel, so we speak, not to please men, but to please God who tests our hearts" (I Thess. 2:3-4). This trust is a personal trust. We are under personal obligation. At the same time, we know it is a corporate trust which we meet together in the Christian Church.

This trust of the gospel is a trust to keep it always fresh, clear and understandable. We are called to continual, earnest searching of its truths, so there can be no mistake about what it is. We are called to respond obediently to its message, so that our lives may demonstrate in full beauty what it means to be reconciled to God and restored into His family. To be entrusted with the gospel is to be continually honoring the Christ, who *is* the gospel in His very person and work. Knowing well the temptations to becloud this precious truth and to bury it under untruth and trivialities, the steward does indeed have an important assignment to keep the gospel clean and pure.

The steward is to love the Christian Church, to make it, in each generation, its most effective best as the vehicle through which the gospel is proclaimed. This is an important part of being entrusted with the gospel and an important part of "serving Him in everlasting righteousness, innocence and blessedness." The Christian steward is not to take his place in the Church simply to be ministered to. He is wrong if his idea of the Christian Church is to consider it as one of many institutions in society. It is the institution through which he can most effectively accomplish his stewardship of the gospel, his proclamation to a dying world of the hope which comes through a risen Christ. Therefore, the steward will give himself and all he has to make the Church the most effective agency it can possibly be. He will strengthen its institutions. He will make use of every opportunity and occasion to reach out into new places and new lives with the preaching of the Word. He will devote himself to the establishing of new congregations. He will be ready and willing to strengthen any section of the Christian Church in the world in order that it may continue to be a base from which the gospel is proclaimed. He will take liberally of what he has in order to make the Church what it ought to be as an effective means for proclaiming God's gracious love.

It should also be said that as one who is entrusted with the gospel, the steward is to explore the strategies by which to bring it to people in each generation. He is to devote himself earnestly to understanding his own times and the relevancy of the eternal revelation to those times. As the circumstances of life vary from one generation to another, so the strategies of proclaiming the gospel will need to vary. The complex social structure of the present age, and the intimate ties between nations, make clear that the strategies for the gospel at this moment must be quite different from the strategies of two or three generations ago. The Christian steward, together with his fellow stewards, is called to apply his best intelligence and his best research to the great Christian proclamation. He will refuse to be a complainer about changes which come, but will rejoice at the signs of dynamic concern, devotion and imagination which are invested in the cause of the gospel.

As a steward with such a holy and awesome trust, he is to devote his available resources to serve this message of God. This means the applying of resources of money, time, ability and all other things that are a part of life. He will discover that all he has is not enough, so he will proceed to encourage others to join with him in the same process of taking available resources to put everything possible into use for Christ and the gospel which is to be proclaimed. The attention which the Christian steward and the Christian Church gives to the matter of money, time and abilities is a valid and legitimate emphasis, if the trust of the gospel is to be taken seriously. Of course, if it is not to be taken seriously, and if Christian people are simply interested in keeping alive some degree of church life for their own sakes or to serve proper social and cultural conventions, then the resources probably do not need to be so very great. If, however, this commission of Christ is to be taken seriously, then there can be no other conclusion but that the steward is called to apply every available means to this high purpose.

*A "guide question" to keep in mind
as you read this chapter:*

**How does the Holy Spirit work—with you
and with others?**


### FOR GROUP DISCUSSION

What, really, is the Christian Church?

How can the church change people's ways of thinking
and acting?

If the individual Christian is "entrusted with the gospel"—why is it said that the Christian Church holds the
Word and Sacraments?

Do you find it a help or a hindrance to be reminded
that you live in the shadow of eternity and have only
a limited number of "mortal years" for your life?

# Chapter Six

# The Steward
# and the Holy Spirit

The Third Article of the Apostolic Creed is the expression of the Church's faith in the person of the Holy Spirit and the work which He does in the hearts of men. We believe in Him as a person equal to the other persons in the Holy Trinity. We do not consider the Holy Spirit to be a force or an influence, but a person actively working and accomplishing the purposes of the Triune God.

The nature of our stewardship is further understood therefore, by our examination of our relationship to the Holy Spirit and His relationship to us. What we are spiritually traces back to Him and to His work. A Christian steward is one who has received the Holy Spirit, is under His guidance and prayerfully seeks to be filled with the Spirit.

### THE THIRD ARTICLE

"I believe in the Holy Ghost; The holy Christian Church, the communion of saints; the forgiveness of sins; the resurrection of the body; and the life everlasting. Amen."

*What does this mean?* I believe that I cannot by my own reason or strength believe in Jesus Christ, my Lord, or come to Him; but the Holy Ghost has called me through the Gospel, enlightened me with His gifts, and sanctified and preserved me in the true faith; in like manner as He calls, gathers, enlightens and sanctifies the whole Christian Church on earth, and preserves it in union with Jesus Christ in the one true faith; in which Christian Church He daily forgives abundantly all my sins, and the sins of all believers, and at the last day will raise up me and all the dead, and will grant everlasting life to me and to all who believe in Christ. This is most certainly true.

Whatever the Christian steward may be, it is clear that the quality of his stewardship is the result of the Spirit's work in his life. The fulfillment of the stewardship which he is able to accomplish is the result of the Spirit's presence. Luther wrote of this when he said—"I believe that I cannot by my own reason or strength believe in Jesus Christ, my Lord, or come to Him; but the Holy Spirit has called me . . . and will grant everlasting life to me and to all who believe in Christ."

Life in all of its forms is created by the Holy Spirit. This was true at the very beginning, at the creation of heaven and earth. It is still true that the Holy Spirit creates life. In this case, He is the creator of spiritual life—trust in Jesus Christ as Savior, and a loving, obedient response to Him. This is not something that man accomplishes, but something which God in His grace and goodness works out in our lives.

The work of the Holy Spirit, through the means of grace, the Word and the Sacraments, is to lead us to know Jesus Christ, to accept Him as our Savior, and to continue in intimate fellowship and association with Him. Luther described this accomplishment when he said—"The Holy Spirit has called me through the gospel, enlightened me with His gifts, and sanctified and preserved me in the true faith; in like manner as He calls, gathers, enlightens, and sanctifies the whole Christian Church on earth, and preserves it in union with

Jesus Christ in the one true faith." In other words, the Christian steward has been called to his stewardship by the Holy Spirit. He has been enlightened through the Word and the Sacraments as a part of the Spirit's work. He has been changed and made holy as a result of the Spirit's being in his life and he has been preserved in his faith as a work of the same Spirit. The Christian steward simply cannot consider himself as being a steward of God, except as a work which has been done in him by this divine person. Stewardship is not an accomplishment of man, it is a divine accomplishment.

The relation of the steward to the Holy Spirit can be understood in part in the words of the Article "I believe in the Holy Spirit, the Holy Christian Church, the communion of saints." The holy Christian Church is the company of people who have been called to Christ by the Holy Spirit and have received the new life, the gift of God in Christ.

There is a great deal of mistaken and shallow thinking on stewardship that is traceable in large measure to superficial ideas and concepts of what the holy Christian Church is and what church membership means. Very often when we speak about the Church, we speak about a building, or we speak about a particular congregation to which we may belong or near which we reside. The strong emphasis upon the prerogatives and rights of a local congregation have often contributed to this limited understanding of the nature of the Church. We recognize that we have church bodies or large church organizations which are made up of many congregations. These church bodies have certain work to which they are committed, certain institutions to be maintained and strengthened and a total corporate life to be watched over. The result of this emphasis on buildings and organization often leads us to think of the Church as something that we join and support largely through the giving of our money for its work. Much understanding of the meaning of Christian stewardship has gone wrong right here. Therefore, it is important that we come to an examination of the phrase—"I believe in the holy Christian Church, the communion of Saints." Perhaps through a serious consideration of what this means, we can get rid of some of the wrong conceptions which have been in the way of our stewardship.

What then is the Christian Church? It is the community of those whom the Holy Spirit has brought into fellowship with the Savior Jesus Christ. The Church in the proper sense is not something which men join, or which they support with their contributions. Its basis is in the work of the Holy Spirit who has called people out of darkness into life. This call is sounded in the forgiveness of sin. The Church, then, is the company of people who have been forgiven, because they have believed in what Christ has done for them.

Probably the most frequently-used word which translated as "church" is the one that signifies a group of people who have been "called out." It is God who has done the calling. It has been His will that has been operative. The members of the holy Christian Church are people whom God has called and chosen, and who as a result have accepted their commission as stewards of His abiding purpose. This concept of the Church as the "called out people" is one which traces directly back into the Old Testament. Israel considered itself the chosen people of God. On this basis it considered itself as being a privileged and specially blessed people among the many nations. The truth which Israel forgot so many times is that along with privilege comes peculiar and special responsibility. The people of Israel overlooked the fact that while they had been called as God's people, they also had been sent to the world to proclaim the love of God.

This is a very important truth for the Christian Church to remember. As a company of those who have been "called out," it holds the position which Israel held. The Christian Church is a company of people who not only have privilege, but who have an important responsibility. They have not only been called, but they have been sent, by God, on an important mission. This is a large part of what the Christian steward is reminded as he recalls that the Holy Spirit has created and called out the Church. It means that the Holy Spirit has assigned responsibility and sent His people on a mission.

The Christian Church has authority and power given to it by God. These are not inherent in it because it is an organization which has good standing in our communities. The authority and power which has been given to it, is to be used in the exercise of its stewardship, and limited to its life as the body of Christ in the world.

Another way in which we can understand the Holy Christian Church and learn our stewardship lessons is by taking a little time to examine the biblical idea that the Church is the body of Christ. (See I Cor. 12:12-31; Ephesians 4:1-16.) This expression is one which has often helped Christian people to understand what the Church is. To describe the Church as the body of Christ is to describe it as active and living, a company of Christian stewards at work in response to their appointment. The life of this community of believers must be nothing less than Christ living in each one of them, and so governing their life and work that He is actually achieving His redeeming purpose in society and among the nations.

When this is characteristic of the Church, then it is most surely not an organization which men join and which they govern according to their own whims and pleasures. It is rather an organism which is possessed by God to accomplish something of eternal value.

When a company of people acts as the body of Christ, so that He is working through them, then its voice will be the voice of the Savior proclaiming His love and invitation. As the body of Christ, its hands will be the hands of our Lord moving about in the world, doing works of love, lifting up the fallen, encouraging the faint-hearted.

As the body of Christ, the Church has many and varied members in the body. So it is in the Christian community. We do not all have the same gifts and abilities nor are we called to do the same work. We fit together under the plan of God. We each have our place and work and mission. We will not want to deride or belittle any member of this Church of Christ, but recognize with thanksgiving the contribution which each can make within his own capacities, spiritual understanding and growth. Every member of a Christian congregation must examine himself at this point in order that he may accept his place and responsibility within the body of Christ.

When we have this concept of the Church as Christ's body, then we can understand that the Church is not present in the world simply to be noticed, but it is here for the doing of the Lord's work. It is present among men to achieve His purposes, that all men shall be saved and come to the knowledge of the truth. This understanding of the Church's reason for existence is the one which should make every steward search his heart and examine his life to the end that he may be a faithful steward and a faithful member of the body.

The steward understands something further of what the Christian Church is through the phrase "the communion of saints." We have already referred to the fact that the true Church is a company of the believers, those who have entered into the forgiveness of sins and the fruits of the resurrection. This communion of saints, as we call it, is a community of people far more intimately knit together than any other community to be found in the world. Its members have been knit together by the work of the Holy Spirit. They are people who are in the process of being sanctified. They know that their great resource is not within themselves, but in the love of a great and glorious God.

When we speak of the communion of saints, we are thinking of the Church as the Church of true believers. Perhaps this is the time to recall however, that the Christian community has, from the beginning, found it necessary and good to establish an organization in a society. We, therefore, have the church within the Church in the sense that the human organization may not be completely the same as the Christians who are a part of it. If the Church of God, however, is to be able to live and work, it must have its organization. It needs a building or buildings. It needs a house and a center from which it can reach out to invite men to come in and to discover the joy and wonder of the gospel. This organized church provides the place where we can offer our children a sound and helpful spiritual home.

The organized Church recognizes the fact that the Christian steward was never intended to live by himself. Christianity is a social manifestation. It is a gathering together of a special group of people who hold special convictions and a special faith.

This insight is an important one for the Christian

steward. He will not be inclined to belittle the organized church. He will be exceedingly grateful for it and for all that it means to the communion of saints. He will recognize that it is within this organized form that the Word and the Sacraments are made available to people and he will rejoice that this is so.

At the same time, he will not be surprised that within the membership of the organized Church there will be those who completely fail to understand the meaning of Christian stewardship. He will not be startled to discover that there are those who are thoroughly unwilling to give of themselves and their means for the cause of the gospel. He will discover it to be a common experience in congregations that selfishness may rule and that the organization is thought of as something totally and completely within the rule of man, rather than under the rule of the redeeming Christ.

A further insight into the significance of the Christian Church and the relation of the steward to it is that the Church is the company of those who are being sanctified. To be sanctified is to be made holy. This is something that man cannot do for himself or to himself. This is something which only the Holy One can accomplish. Fredrik Wisloff writes:

> "We are so inclined to think like this: In His boundless grace God has saved me; now I must see to it that I become holy. God has done His part, now I must do mine. The least I can do is to take hold of the work of sanctification with an upright mind and undivided will."
>
> Fredrik Wisløff, "I Believe in the Holy Spirit."

This, Dr. Wisloff says, is the way we so easily think. The fact is that we cannot make ourselves holy. We cannot change our lives for good. That is something which the Spirit must do in us. That is a fruit of His grace. God is the one who takes action. We are the ones that are acted upon. It is perfectly clear why this is an important truth for the Christian steward, for stewardship is a matter of sanctification. To live life responsibly as a child of God calls for some great transformations to take place in our wills and hearts. This transformation we cannot produce on our own. That is a divine work.

Growth in responsible stewardship is a part of being sanctified. We must expect this change to come only as people live under the work of the Holy Spirit. Since we know that the Spirit of God works through the Word of God and the Sacraments, this means that lives will be changed in the area of stewardship only through exposure to the Word and by participation in the Sacraments. We may be able, in a congregation, to create something of a helpful climate, but we cannot produce the change in any other way.

Very often the best response in stewardship is dependent upon the degree of spiritual maturity of the Christian. It may not mean that a person is not a Christian because he does not thoroughly understand what is expected of the Christian steward. It may rather be that he is very much of a babe in Christ and needs the assistance of his Christian brothers to grow to maturity and responsibility.

The relationship of the steward to the Holy Spirit is also understood in part in the words of this Third Article—"I believe—in the forgiveness of sins, the resurrection of the body and the life everlasting." Luther described these blessings as the work of the Holy Spirit; "at the last day He will raise up me and all the dead, and will grant everlasting life to me and to all who believe in Christ. This is most certainly true."

It is not necessary at this point to discuss what we mean by the forgiveness of sins. This has already been discussed in connection with the Second Article. The important fact to remember is that it is the Holy Spirit who brings about the forgiveness of sins. He is the Person who calls man to give attention to Jesus Christ and the redemptive work which He has accomplished. The steward will do well to remember that his life in Christ and his faith in the forgiveness of sins is something that has been done in him and for him. It is not something for which he takes credit. It is not a state which makes him a better man than another. The fact of what the Holy Spirit had done is to keep the steward in deep humility, knowing that everything he is and everything he can proclaim has been brought about by God whose steward he is. In one sense, he is himself of no value. In another sense, because he has been called to be a steward, he has value beyond comprehension.

As the steward remembers that it is the Holy Spirit who leads him into the forgiveness of sin, he will be alerted to the great tragedy that every sin is. Every sin serves to cut off the sinner from the flow of life into him from God. It can produce, and does produce, very serious injury to him as a member of the body of Christ. He cannot function properly until he is healed and restored and made a living member again. The fact that the Holy Spirit brings man into this forgiveness is further cause for the steward to live in utter and complete thankfulness for His work.

The steward also recognizes in the work of the Holy Spirit the fact that Scripture says there is to be a resurrection of the body and everlasting life. This is a great and glorious promise for the time when the stewardship of these mortal years is concluded. The assurance that it is to be accomplished lies in the fact that this too is the work of the Holy Spirit, the great life-giver. Even as He gave life in the beginning, and does now give spiritual life to us, so also He most surely will give that everlasting life which will come into being as a result of the resurrection. This fact gives confidence and purpose to the steward as he seeks to serve the God who has called him and appointed him.

## IN CONCLUSION

The Apostolic Creed, which we have been reviewing, is an important focal point, indeed, for the Christian steward. In the First Article, his faith in God the Father brings him to an understanding of the extent and nature of his stewardship, and of the intimate ties which exist between him and the God who is his Creator.

His faith in God the Son brings him to the centrality of the Cross and the importance of the forgiveness of sin. Out of these truths arises the whole motivation for his stewardship. His faith in God the Spirit, highlighted in the Third Article, brings him to the assurance of God's plan to make him a part of His holy Christian Church and to equip him in that fellowship for the stewardship to which he has been called. Truly, we are stewards by God's decision and appointment.

*A "guide question" to keep in mind
as you read this chapter:*

**Why pray, since God knows all about it anyway?**

## FOR GROUP DISCUSSION

What really is "a praying person"?

When is it right for the Christian steward to destroy?

When an individual prays the Lord's Prayer, should not the plural pronouns be changed to singular?

What proportion of the temptations people face are temptations in the matter of stewardship?

# Chapter Seven

# The Steward Prays

The Christian steward prays as a member of God's family. He is on the kind of an assignment in the world which he could not possibly accomplish by himself. He is desperately in need of constant communication with the One who has appointed him. Through prayer he opens his heart and life for God's forgiveness, for the wisdom which He would impart and for that work of the Holy Spirit which will make him more and more a sanctified and holy person. As he prays, it is most natural that he should move beyond request for himself to an encompassing concern for all that concerns God himself.

The steward who does not pray, or who is less and less inclined to pray, will quickly find himself separated from God. The entire concept of relationship of the steward to God makes it unthinkable that the steward would not be a praying person

It is our intention in this chapter to explore the prayer life of the steward through the prayer lessons of Jesus, which are incorporated in the Lord's Prayer. These are the prayers which He taught to His disciples.

### THE INTRODUCTION

"Our Father who art in heaven."

*What does this mean?* God thereby tenderly encourages us to believe that He is truly our Father, and that we are truly

His children, so that we may boldly and confidently come to Him in prayer, even as beloved children come to their dear father.

It is exceedingly significant that as Jesus teaches the steward to pray He uses the plural. There are several lessons which the word "our" gives us as we consider this opening phrase of the Prayer. For one thing, this is a reminder that we are member's of God's family and that God has many children. We ought to stop long enough to remember who some of those children are, what their needs are, what their witness means to us and to the whole cause of the gospel. When the steward prays, he does it with his arms stretched out around his Christian brothers and says "Our Father."

This word in the plural is a prayer for the Christian Church. The Church includes those who are the members of God's family, but just to use the word "our" involves us in every pulpit, in every church classroom, and educational program, in every charitable institution, in the political and economic circumstances which affect the life and work of the Christian Church. We cannot properly pray as Christian stewards without remembering the Church at all points and in all circumstances.

To use the plural is to remember that we are real sons and daughters of God. If this is so, then we do not expect to be pampered. We expect to be treated as responsible and mature members of the family. We discover quickly enough that the family of God is a family of cross-bearers. To say "Our" is to review quickly in our hearts the selfless devotion and unmitigated courage which we are called upon to demonstrate in our stewardship. Of course, the need for this cross-bearing varies according to the generation in which we live and the situation in our homeland. But we are quite sure when we throw our arms out around our fellow stewards, that there are multitudes who have given a stewardship witness far beyond anything we might have brought.

To understand the path of prayer into which Christ is leading, we want to take note of the word "Father." Luther in his explanation pointed out for us that this word is to make us sure about something—"that we may boldly and confidently come to Him in prayer, even as beloved children come to their dear father." Surely this is the spirit in which the steward prays. We are true children. We have the privilege of direct access to Him. We can tell Him exactly what is on our heart and share with Him the perplexities of our stewardship. The way is completely open, no man need ever doubt that this is so.

In these opening words, we also note "who art in heaven." We as stewards are ruled by the conditions in life upon this earth, but this Father is not ruled by these conditions. He is not as bound by circumstances as we are. He rules circumstances.

## THE FIRST PETITION

"Hallowed be Thy Name."

*What does this mean?* God's Name is indeed holy in itself; but we pray in this petition that it may be hallowed also among us.

*How is this done?* When the Word of God is taught in its truth and purity, and we, as God's children, lead holy lives, in accordance with it. This grant us, dear Father in heaven! But whoever teaches and lives otherwise than as God's Word teaches, profanes the Name of God among us. From this preserve us, heavenly Father!

In this section of the Prayer, which we call the First Petition, there is an echo from the Second Command-

ment. Both of them deal with the importance and place
of the Name of God. It is worth noting how Luther
explained this Prayer—"we pray that it may be hallowed
also among us." The Christian steward is very much
aware, or at least he ought to be, that the name of God
needs to be hallowed in his own heart and life. Unless
it has this holiness about it, unless God is recognized as
the One before whom the angels veil their faces, it is
quite possible for the steward to treat his stewardship
very lightly. It is only as he is called and recalled to
examine the reality of God in His holiness and justice
that he is going to keep the proper sense of his stewardship. Furthermore, he knows, or he ought to know, that
the Christian Church needs to have the name of God
hallowed. This community of believers can very easily
be led astray into an overevaluation of themselves and
an underevaluation of the Triune God. It is necessary
for the health of the Church that the name of God shall
be held sacred among us. This prayer is a cry of adoring
awe, a recognition of God in the light of His revelation.

Luther raises the question, "how do we go about hallowing and honoring and adoring the name of God?" He
answers it in these simple words—"When the Word of
God is taught in its truth and purity, and we, as God's
children, lead holy lives, in accordance with it." The
prayer of the steward fervently and earnestly poured
out certainly implies that he will devote himself to the
hallowing of God's name if he understands how to do
it. Therefore, the steward is committed to the teaching
of the Word of God in its truth and purity. This is
where men come to know God. This is where He reveals himself. This is the source of all that the world
knows about Him. If there is to be hallowing of the
name of God, it must rise out of this ground. Further-

more, as we are reminded, this honoring of His name
will be accomplished by Christian stewards as they live
lives that are in accordance with what the Bible says
a godly life should be. The importance that is given
in this explanation to the teaching of the Word in its
truth and purity should be noted carefully. When false
ideas or impressions get into the teaching, when human
philosophy is mixed with the revelation, then it is easy
to lose the knowledge of the true nature and love of
God. The steward who prays this prayer dedicates himself to an important mission which involves the revealed
Word.

## THE SECOND PETITION

"Thy kingdom come."

*What does this mean?* The kingdom of God comes indeed
of itself, without our prayer; but we pray in this petition
that it may also come to us.

*How is this done?* When our heavenly Father gives us His
Holy Spirit, so that by His grace we believe His holy Word,
and live a godly life here on earth, and in heaven forever.

When we pray this Prayer, we remember that the
kingdom is God's kingdom. It is where Jesus Christ, His
Son, reigns. This kingdom is not the creation of man,
it is the gift of God. We have no right to glory in any
aspect of it. We have every right to wonder and rejoice at its nature, its people and its king. To enter this
kingdom, is God's gift. To live in the kingdom is possible by His love and His goodness.

When Luther explained this petition, he said "we
pray that it may come also to us." In other words, we
pray that this gift which is His kingdom will be given
to us and to all of those who are included in our prayer.

Certainly, when we pray "Thy kingdom come," we

are praying for ourselves as Christian stewards. To desire His kingdom to come in ourselves and in our lives, this is the prayer of the Christian for himself. We pray here that the day will come soon when the God-pleasing things we do, now so few, will be increased many-fold. It is a recognition of how poorly equipped our lives are and how little Jesus actually reigns in our motives and deeds.

This petition is intended, certainly, to include a prayer for the whole company of believers which we call the Christian Church. Very often we express ourselves as though the Kingdom of God and the visible Christian Church are one and the same. We go as far as to say that "we are building the kingdom." Obviously, this is not the meaning that can be in this prayer. We do not build the kingdom. God does. Our prayer is that it may come in us, and that within the hearts of His children He may more and more direct their lives to the fulfilling of His purposes.

This Prayer is most certainly a prayer that the kingdom of God will come in the world. This is the mission prayer of the Christian steward. It is the prayer for the unsaved all around us. It is a prayer for America and for all the nations. It is a prayer that implies the need of God's care for all the people and all the institutions who are doing His work and going forth in his name.

This is a prayer that implies the readiness of the steward to support the mission, the educational, and the charitable work of His church. It puts him on record as earnestly desiring that everything which will cause the kingdom to come will be done, will be prospered and will be supported to the fullest extent possible. This prayer records a steward as having seen the great harvest fields of God.

This prayer goes beyond the kingdom in human hearts, which shall be in this world. It is a prayer for the triumphant and eternal kingdom to come. This involves the expectation of the return of our Lord to usher in a new heaven and a new earth. This is the climax of His kingdom! Our prayer here is for the full and final accomplishment of that which God has planned for His created world. This petition of the steward enables him to look beyond the responsibilities and opportunities of the moment, to the assurances which are ever present in the Christian message.

Luther's words remind us that this Prayer is answered when our Heavenly Father gives us His Spirit, and when the Spirit of God brings us to faith in His Holy Word and works in us godly living. In other words, the coming of the kingdom is not a great mystery. We know how it comes. It is only necessary for us to see to it that the work of the Spirit may be prospered among us.

### THE THIRD PETITION

"Thy will be done on earth as it is in heaven."

*What does this mean?* The good and gracious will of God is done indeed without our prayer; but we pray in this petition that it may also be done among us.

*How is this done?* When God destroys and brings to naught every evil counsel and purpose of the devil, the world, and our own flesh, which would hinder us from hallowing His name, and prevent the coming of His kingdom; and when he strengthens us and keeps us steadfast in His Word and in faith, even unto our end. This is His good and gracious will.

We know some things about the will of God. We know that it is always good. We know that it is absolutely perfect. We know it is sovereign, that it does not yield to any other person. We know it is righteous and holy and glorious. We understand that the chief part of the Father's will, as we find it in the Scripture, is "that all men shall be saved and come to the knowledge of the truth."

When we begin to examine what we know about God's will, we discover that He has made up His mind about many things. Above everything else He has made up His mind that men are to be saved and that their salvation is to be brought about now and is to be effective for eternity. It is possible to frustrate the will of God, but His intentions are perfectly clear.

When we pray "thy will be done" we recognize that there are other wills and other intentions which also affect man. We usually speak of these as the will of the devil, the world and our flesh. The prayer of the steward is that these wills or intentions will not succeed, but that God will have His way.

We come to know the will of God when we are really willing to see to it that His purposes are carried out and, furthermore, that our own lives will fit into those purposes. To know God's will, there must be a willingness to submit ourselves and our purposes to Him. This ought not to be unusual for the person who has committed himself as a steward of God. Therefore, this is a proper and natural prayer for the Christian steward.

In Luther's explanation of how this is done, he pointed out that the will of God is done first by bringing destruction to all of those things that stand in the way of His will. Then He accomplishes it by strengthening us and keeping us firmly established in His Word and in our faith as long as we live. To pray that He will have things work out the way He wants, is to pray that all evil purposes will be defeated and that His strengthening will take place in every man.

This has never been an easy prayer for an honest man to pray. The dominance of our own desires and intentions is well known to all of us. This prayer begins by acknowledging that wherever there is a difference, God is right and we are wrong. The steward does not make his own rules. He does not cut out his own patterns. He is in this world to serve the will of God. This means that his primary purpose is to see to it that all men shall be saved and come to the knowledge of the truth. This calls for more than lip service. It calls for the complete and unreserved dedication of all the material and spiritual forces which one can marshals to accomplish this. To pray this prayer is to burn our personal bridges behind us; it is to commit our lives and our means.

## THE FOURTH PETITION

"Give us this day our daily bread."

*What does this mean?* God indeed gives daily bread to all men, even to the wicked, without our prayer; but we pray in this petition that He would lead us to acknowledge our daily bread as His gift, and to receive it with thanksgiving.

*What is meant by daily bread?* Everything that is required to satisfy our bodily needs; such as food and raiment, house and home, fields and flocks, money and goods; pious parents, children and servants; godly and faithful rulers, good government, seasonable weather, peace and health; order and honor; true friends, good neighbors, and the like.

In the preceding three Petitions, the Lord has taught us to offer prayers which concern God's name, God's kingdom and God's will. In this prayer, we place particular needs before God. This is a prayer for the necessities of life. It can never be understood to be a prayer for the luxuries which we might desire.

When the Christian steward prays for daily bread,

he does it as he recalls the words—"A man's life consisteth not in the abundance of the things which he possesses." We are not to become unusually concerned about this petition, but at the same time to remember that we have a right to pray it in order that we might sustain life as we set forth to serve and glorify God. We ask for daily bread because we are God's stewards, because we have this highly important purpose to accomplish.

It is also to be recognized that in this prayer the plural pronoun shows up again. We pray "give us . . ." This is no invitation to think solely about ourselves. If we imagine that we have no responsibility for the daily bread of others, then we are completely wrong. In the case of food and all the other necessities of life, we stand in a human chain. We accept these things from others, but we are also responsible for passing these things along; for the needs of some are the needs of us all.

Perhaps we ought to recall here that the Christian does not pray this prayer in order that he may eat, but in order that he may live. This, of course, raises the question as to what is the purpose of life. The steward knows full well what the purpose of life is. It is to serve God, and to do this with the same overflowing love that is in God Himself. To ask God for daily bread is to ask Him for another day in which to serve Him.

It does not seem to stretch the meaning of this petition to find in it our guidance for all genuine Christian economics, for that organization of society which concerns itself with providing for the necessities of a people. To pray intelligently in this petition is to acknowledge that we need the kind of society in which men may have enough for their needs. In uttering the prayer, we commit ourselves to the kind of stewardship of life and intelligence which may bring this about more completely than we have ever known it.

It should be added that this prayer for daily bread assumes that we are not seeking to get it by means which are displeasing to God, or for purposes which cannot have His blessing. We know very well there are great numbers of people who get what they need without very much concern about how they get it. Their practices in business, their readiness to speculate and gamble and use other illegal and immoral methods make perfectly clear that they are willing to take into their own hands the providing of their daily bread. We also recognize that there is a considerable company of people who see to it that the earnings they make are set in reserve for themselves. This accumulated wealth is seen as a way of meeting personal needs and providing for personal luxuries, even though the Christian Church is in need of much more than it has to wage its battle against an evil world. To get daily bread without recognition of obligation is to demonstrate a complete lack of understanding as to why we are here and how we are to use the material world.

Certainly this whole state of mind and heart which has been referred to above underlines the way that Luther explained this petition—"We pray that He would lead us to acknowledge our daily bread as His gift and to receive it with thanksgiving." This thanksgiving reveals itself in the whole quality of life and the dedication to our stewardship purposes.

## THE FIFTH PETITION

"And forgive us our trespasses, as we forgive those who trespass against us."

*What does this mean?* We pray in this petition that our

heavenly Father would not regard our sins nor because of them deny our prayers; for we neither merit, nor deserve those things for which we pray; but that He would grant us all things through grace, even though we sin daily, and deserve nothing but punishment. And certainly we, on our part, will heartily forgive, and gladly do good to those who may sin against us.

In this petition we come to familiar ground, which we have noted in other sections of our study. We have been reminded in several places that the forgiveness of sin is at the heart of the steward's relationship to God. Here Jesus is teaching us to pray for the forgiveness of our sins, and telling us that we are also to forgive the sins of others. Perhaps this is the point at which we could recognize that human sin is far more than a particular act or series of acts. It is a general human condition and no one of us is exempt from the condition. It is a state of our nature, which produces one kind of sin and then another. The steward will never be through praying for forgiveness. It will be and must be a part of every day's experience. A Christian steward can never be anything else but a repentant sinner. If he is an unrepentant sinner, he is quickly set aside from his stewardship. The two cannot be joined together.

This prayer for forgiveness also includes the plural pronoun. Jesus teaches us to pray "and forgive us." It should not be our attitude that we are praying only for our own forgiveness. This is a point at which we remember all men. We will look with full understanding at the tragedy of their lives, because we know the tragedy of our own. To make this prayer a prayer which includes others will help us to move temperately, thoughtfully and generously in all of our human relationships. Jesus is helping us at a most important point when He teaches us to bring our sins to God in this manner. As we strike this note in our prayer, we also understand that we are praying for God's forgiveness of our corporate or group sins. We are asking Him to forgive the sins of the Christian Church and the sins of society and the sins of the nation to which we belong. Just as surely as we understand the evil of our own hearts, the nature which wants to control us, so we understand the moral and spiritual state of the groups in our social structure. We ought not to set these relationships aside as though they are in a completely separate category. The fact is that Jesus teaches us to pray for forgiveness across all the areas of life. The Christian steward is well advised to understand this and to pray in this manner. The life which he is called upon to live will always be in a setting of sin and rebellion. He must expect this. He must conduct himself accordingly. He must carry the spirit of God with him in all of his associations, in the Church and beyond it.

## THE SIXTH PETITION

"And lead us not into temptation."

*What does this mean?* God indeed tempts no one to sin; but we pray in this petition that God would so guard and preserve us, that the devil, the world, and our own flesh may not deceive us, nor lead us into error and unbelief, despair, and other great and shameful sins; but that, when so tempted, we may finally prevail and gain the victory.

As soon as we pass from the petition which calls us to confess our sins, Jesus teaches us to pray to our Heavenly Father about the possibility of future sin. We certainly know that temptations will be ahead of us. The fact that the steward may pray this prayer is a part of his assurance that God will be at his side and His strength will be available when the temptations come. We are not going to permit ourselves to be fooled about the kind of world in which we live; but neither are we going to permit ourselves to go unarmed and alone. The steward will recognize his weakness and his spiritual frailty. He will prepare for that which can defeat him and destroy him.

Perhaps it is a valid point to recognize that when the Christian steward really tries to give himself earnestly and courageously to the service of God, he may move into situations which will produce the greatest temptation. We seem to find constantly that in any given circumstance we have the possibility of serving God; but there is inevitable temptation that goes along with it. This prayer is the response of the steward to this fact. He does not want to withdraw from the complete outpouring of himself in the service of God, but he does know that he must have God with him in these ventures which he is called upon to make.

The steward will also be reminded in this prayer lesson of Christ that he ought not to walk into temptation. He ought to be wise enough to avoid the situations which probably will cause him to sin. This point of view on his part would not be the conclusion of a coward, but would be the evaluation of the wise man who knows himself and knows the powers of evil to be very real.

## THE SEVENTH PETITION

"But deliver us from evil."

*What does this mean?* We pray in this petition, as in a summary, that our heavenly Father would deliver us from all manner of evil, whether it affect the body or soul, property or reputation, and at last, when the hours of death shall come, grant us a blessed end, and graciously take us from this world of sorrow to Himself in heaven.

This petition, as Luther has pointed out, is a kind of summary. It is a prayer that God would deliver us from evil, not solely by leading us away from it, but by enabling us to deal with it. The experience of Christian people certainly says that one important way to be delivered from evil is to fill our lives with that which is good. We meet the evil by filling our hearts with the Word of God. We meet it with the Sacraments. We meet it in the Communion of Saints. We meet it as we steep ourselves in the whole Christian heritage.

When we pray this prayer, as Christian stewards, it represents our longing for freedom from sin and from all the evil results of sin, which we know are abroad in the world. It is the pouring out of our hearts to our Heavenly Father that the warfare may be finally accomplished, that our stewardship may be victoriously and fruitfully completed and that we may find our eternal place with God Himself where no evil can ever come.

At the same time that this note of weariness in the conflict is in the prayer there is a confident faith that our prayer will be answered. We count on our Father in Heaven. We know that He hears us and we know that His answer will be good and complete, for we say "Thine is the kingdom, and the power, and the glory, forever and ever. Amen."

*A "guide question" to keep in mind
as you read this chapter:*

From the general attitudes held by the people
of your congregation, what do you think little
children are learning about baptism?

## FOR GROUP DISCUSSION

In what ways are baptism and adoption similar?

What does your congregation do, as a follow-up to holy
baptism?

Is it important to have baptism as a public event?

Do the little children of your congregation have an opportunity to *see* baptism regularly?

# Chapter Eight

# The Steward
# and the Sacrament of Baptism

It has been noted in the preceding chapters that we
are not conducting a full scale study of all the meaning
which is packed into the Commandments, the Creed,
and the Lord's Prayer. We are rather making the kind
of study which will help us *as Christian stewards* to review some lessons and gain some insights which are
inherent in the Christian faith. This principle is to be
applied further to the subject which is now at hand.
There are exceedingly important insights into the Sacraments which could and would take us far afield from
our basic purpose. It is the intention in this chapter,
as in the others, to seek out those insights which will
throw light on the meaning of the stewardship of the
Christian man. We have noted in earlier pages the strategic place of the Sacraments in the life of the Christian
Church, and therefore, in the life of the individual
Christian. The Sacraments, together with the Word of
God, are the means of grace for us. We call them this
because the scriptural records tell us that through Baptism, and the partaking of the Lord's Supper, we receive
the forgiveness of sins. This is the grace of God coming
to man. These are the means that He uses. These are
the visible vehicles by which He reaches us.

**Furthermore**, the Sacraments are strategic in our life

because they are involved in our entrance into our stewardship and are important for our spiritual growth and our development.

Tanner, in his instruction book for confirmation, reminds us that the Sacraments meet the needs of God's children. He says:

"Having received God's forgiveness over and over again, we at times find it difficult to believe that God loves and forgives us even today. Now it is this fact that He loves and forgives us even today that God wants us firmly to believe. Our peace, joy, strength and victory depend upon a firm faith in God's love and forgiveness. So Christ gave the Sacraments, where He deals with each one in a special and personal manner."

Jacob Tanner, "Senior Confirmation Book," APH.

Certainly the steward, given great responsibility and living in a most significant relationship should be aware that he can be dealt with in a special and personal way. The Sacraments become for him highly important meeting places with his God.

## THE SACRAMENT OF BAPTISM

### I

*"What is Baptism?"* Baptism is not simply water, but it is the water used according to God's command and connected with God's Word.

*"What is this Word of God?"* It is the word of our Lord Jesus Christ, as recorded in the last chapter of Matthew:

"Go ye therefore and make disciples of all nations, baptizing them into the Name of the Father, and of the Son, and of the Holy Spirit."

### II

*"What gifts or benefits does Baptism bestow?"* It works forgiveness of sins, delivers from death and the devil, and

gives everlasting salvation to all who believe, as the word and promise of God declares.

*"What is this word and promise of God?"* It is the word of our Lord Jesus Christ, as recorded in the last chapter of Mark:

"He that believeth and is baptized shall be saved; but he that believeth not shall be damned."

In Baptism, the steward is born into his stewardship. This is where and how it all begins. His Baptism will therefore be a continual point of reference. When doubts arise about the purpose of his life, this will be his reassurance. That which happens in Baptism is a reminder that we did not choose this office and relationship for ourselves. Christ has chosen us. Baptism is a gift to mankind. It is the act whereby God lays claim to us.

The Scripture says that in Baptism a person experiences the new birth. He is born again of water and the Spirit. When this happens, there are benefits which come to the person who is baptized. Luther, in his explanation has reminded us that these benefits are that "it works forgiveness of sins, delivers from death and the devil, and gives everlasting salvation to all who believe, as the word and promise of God declares." These are benefits without which no man could be a steward of God. Without forgiveness and deliverance and assurance of everlasting salvation, a man would be completely out of his proper place and unable to move about as a representative of God and in His service.

In Baptism, a person is made a member of God's family. Perhaps we can understand what this means by thinking of a child being adopted into a royal family. The duty and right of royalty will be upon him. At the time of his adoption this will mean nothing to him. As he grows up in the royal household, he will gradually come to understand what this means. The full impact of his royal status will not come until and unless the crown is placed upon his own head. This is what it means to be made a member of the royal family of God. It is a distinct and peculiar position. When a person comes to grasp the truth of it, even in part, he can never really be the same again. The stamp of special responsibility and privilege has been placed upon his life.

The steward who has been adopted into this family through Baptism must go through the experience which the member of the royal family goes through. An education process begins which continues through his lifetime. The implications of his position and responsibility will grow with the passing of the years. A process of enlightenment will be taking place in which the Holy Spirit will be present. It is important for us in the Christian Church to understand that this learning process must take place for the Christian steward. There are times when it is implied that because a person is a Christian, a member of God's family, he is fully equipped and ready at the point of stewardship. The facts are completely contrary to this, of course. The process of enlightenment is necessary, for we discover that without it certain aspects of our stewardship responsibility can be completely ignored or thoroughly misunderstood. There are Christian people who give evidence of quite a varied maturity in these matters, whether it is a question of the stewardship of money, or of time, or talents, or whatever their resources may be.

The Christian Church has responsibility for the training of the baptized person. The Church must see to it that children are reached with instruction in the essentials of Christian faith and life. Obligations are placed on the church that baptizes, and upon the parents who

bring the child for baptism. The child is to be set in
the midst of the church's love, and prayers, and work.
The need for warm, loving support in the process of
maturing is clearly evident to all who know children.

The importance of enlightenment of the baptized
person is underscored in the closing verses of Matthew's
Gospel, where Jesus is recorded as saying—"Go therefore,
and make disciples of all nations, baptizing them in the
Name of the Father and of the Son and of the Holy
Spirit, teaching them to observe all that I have commanded you, and lo, I am with you always to the close
of the age." In these words, Jesus joins together the importance of baptizing and of teaching. It goes without
saying that a part of the teaching which will be done
is the meaning of this great commission itself, with what
it says of the dimensions of stewardship. The baptized
person as a member of God's royal family, is destined
to go and to make disciples among the nations. He will
deny his spiritual birthright unless he makes this use
of his life.

In baptism, God makes a covenant or agreement with
us. We do not embark upon our responsibilities in the
family of God as lonesome and isolated venturers. The
fact that God has made some promises to us places good
foundations under our stewardship. He has promised
that we are His and will be kept by His Spirit. He promises the forgiveness of sins and a readiness on His part to
stand with continual forgiveness and strengthening. He
assures us that we can draw on Him for all our needs,
that His love and grace and goodness are forever available. He invites us to make use of the boundless stores
of strengthening and care which are His. He assures
us that we may take refuge in Him when sin and doubt
and failure wait at our door. The baptismal covenant

is one of the great treasures of the Christian steward. He is not on his own. He is not adrift on a stormy sea. He belongs to God, and God will never forsake him.

It is very important for the Christian steward to understand that in his baptism it was God Himself who was working. Man is passive in baptism. This is not something which we perform and in which we can take pride. We are the object of the love of God and the object of His forgiveness. An important part of what happens, according to God's plan, is that the Holy Spirit enters into us. He dwells in our hearts. We are the house where He lives. When the Holy Spirit abides in us, then He proceeds to do that which is always His purpose and program. He proceeds to teach us and to reveal Jesus Christ. He proceeds to guide us into all truth, so that we are not frantic wanderers amidst the ideas, philosophies and perversions of man. The steward looks at this miraculous event in wonder at what God has done. He does not fully understand what has happened, but he does know that the Triune God has met him at a moment that is personally unique, laid claim to him, and established an eternal covenant with him. The significance of his position cannot be mistaken.

Baptism is an act which ordinarily takes place in the midst of the Christian congregation and people are aware that it is taking place. This is exceedingly important. Baptism is a public event. It is the occasion for the grafting of another member into the visible body of Christ. It is a way of saying publicly that the claim of Christ on this person has over-ruled the claim of Satan, and that it is the intention of God and His people to retain this member in the body. This fact concerning Baptism is important to the Christian steward also. His stewardship is on record. The Church knows that he is committed to being a member of the body of Christ. He cannot deny this in private. His denial would be recognized by the whole Christian community for what it is. At the same time, his faithfulness will bring joy and courage to the Christian congregation.

In Baptism, God gives the Christian steward his life's program. He does not need to create that for himself. The God who has received him into His family knows what He wants to do in him and through him. When we are baptized, we are given, for the period of our whole life, grace and responsibility. Those two cannot be separated and they must not be. If we were only given responsibility in Baptism, we would break under the burden. It simply could not be met. If we were only given forgiveness and salvation, without being made responsible, our lives could fritter away in uselessness. Therefore, when we enter into the family which is the kingdom of God, we are made responsible persons. We are given work to do and purposes to accomplish.

As we confront the program of God for our lives, we are quickly aware that this is no simple assignment. We find a battle within our own hearts. There is evil desire and there is love for God. Both are present. Conflict exists between these two. The Christian steward is in the center of this conflict. He experiences a daily fight for renewal of his baptismal relationship to God. In this fight, he is not alone. The Spirit of God does battle for him in order that the old nature can be defeated and subdued and the new nature can rule. Our response to our God-given program must recognize this fact. The Christian steward is well advised to understand this about himself. In one sense, he can never change from the sinful man that he is. He is destined to defeat and trouble. In another sense, he can continually be a different man. He is destined to live to the glory of God.

What is the character of the program that God gives to His baptized children, to His stewards? This is not the point at which to attempt a thorough definition of it, but such things as the following are included. The simplest way to say it is to say that the steward is committed to God's plan and desire for the world. He is committed to God's will. Whatever his occupation will be, or his place in society will become, this will be his basic responsibility. It will give primary direction to his life.

It will also be a part of his life's program that he shall develop to the utmost the inner resources which God has given to him. His intellectual equipment, his moral insights, his Christian faith and all the potentialities which are his as a person—all these are committed to this program. He is called to bring to it the best he is and the best he has. He ought not to settle for using one talent when he has ten. The program that confronts the Christian steward calls for the unreserved use of all that God has made available to him.

This program of the Christian steward certainly includes dominion over the created world, and a responsible place in human society. However, since he is who he is in the sight of God, he will exercise his dominion and meet his responsibilities in society as a spiritually reborn person. The whole conviction, commitment, and orientation of his life will be around God, around the Cross of Jesus Christ, around forgiveness and the restoration which the Spirit can give. The measurement of his responsibility as a citizen in the world of men will be determined as he daily finds his place in the kingdom of God.

This program for the steward will give high place to the Christian Church, its life, its faith and its program. He will recognize that the Christian Church, for all of the faults that may show up in its members, is the institution and community of people which has been entrusted with the Gospel of life and salvation. The Christian steward will love the Church and devote himself to it. At the same time he will seek to respond to the whole breadth of the responsibilities of life which are his as a child of God.

*A "guide question" to keep in mind*
*as you read this chapter:*

> **What really does communion mean to the
> people of your congregation?**

### FOR GROUP DISCUSSION

Does the confession of sins in the communion service of
your congregation seem to be a "public dying" or
throwing away of false fronts?

In there some feeling, in your congregation, that receiving communion requires a special degree of worthiness?

What does holy communion mean to you?

# Chapter Nine

# The Steward
# and the Sacrament of the Altar

*What is the Sacrament of the Altar?* It is the true Body and Blood of our Lord Jesus Christ, under the bread and wine, given unto us Christians to eat and to drink, as it was instituted by Christ Himself.

*Where is it so written?* The holy Evangelists, Matthew, Mark and Luke, together with St. Paul, writes thus:

"Our Lord Jesus Christ, in the night in which he was betrayed, took bread; and when he had given thanks, he brake it and gave it to his disciples, saying, Take, eat; this is my body, which is given for you; this do in remembrance of me."

"After the same manner also he took the cup, when he had supped, and when he had given thanks, he gave it to them, saying, Drink ye all of it; this cup is the new testament in my blood, which is shed for you, and for many, for the remission of sins; this do, as oft as ye drink it, in remembrance of me."

*What is the benefit of such eating and drinking?* It is pointed out in these words:

"Given and shed for you for the remission of sins." Through these words the remission of sins, life and salvation are given unto us in the sacrament; for where there is remission of sins, there is also life and salvation.

The Christian steward who is in this world on an important mission, responsible to his Eternal God, is brought to confession of sin in the Sacrament of the Altar, or the Lord's Supper, as it is also called. While this will certainly not be a pleasant experience—to confront the necessity and importance of confession of sin—nevertheless, for the steward, it is an absolute essential if he is to maintain communication with his God and Lord.

Since the Sacrament of the Altar has as its basic gift and blessing the forgiveness of sins, it is implied in the very act of participation that the communicant recognizes his need of forgiveness and is willing to admit the reason. This is a place in his spiritual life where all sham must be ended. At this moment he is in the presence of Christ in a special way. God is dealing with him in very personal terms. The steward needs the kind of public acknowledgement of sin, of need, and of the cross of Jesus, which is at the heart of this holy experience. It is a kind of public dying which takes place in him.

When we stay in isolation with our sin, and do not confess it or expose it in the presence of other Christian people, we become more and more involved in it and enslaved by it. The sin becomes more and more destructive because we will not admit its presence and its effect. To confess our sin, as is implied in receiving the Sacrament, is to get at our pride. It brings the fact of what we are out into the open. There is no further room for pretense. When this action on our part is done in the midst of our Christian brothers and neighbors, it means that we are throwing away all of the false front we may have attempted to maintain in their presence.

In admitting that we are sinful, both as to our nature and as to the record of our life, we can then break with the past. Not until we are willing to admit our failure can we make this break. When we do, a dominion and an enslavement is broken. We break through our desperate situation to certainty of the complete competence of God to deal with it. We break through to forgiveness, to love, to true communion with God.

The confession which is involved in the Sacrament straightens out our attitudes toward our fellow Christian stewards. Their very worst sins and failures no longer surprise us. We have seen too deeply into the rebellion of our own heart to be startled at any kind of evidence of the rebellion and the evil which may be in theirs. This, too, is an important experience for the Christian steward. He must not carry within him a sense of superiority over against his fellow stewards, but recognize that, together, we are very mortal men who have been called to serve as appointees of a God who loves and forgives and restores every one.

Of course, the steward receives something much more than the occasion for the confession of his sins when he comes to this Holy Supper. He also experiences joy in what he receives in the Sacrament. He remembers what God has done about forgiving sin. The words of institution say "this do in remembrance of me." The Body and Blood of Christ received in and with the bread and wine are to make the steward remember something and to remember someone. This is a special moment in the flow of the Christian life and the fellowship of the Christian Church. In this moment our minds and hearts are called to full attention to the person of Jesus. We remember who He is and what He has done. Furthermore, we remember that it is God alone who is acting and working in the Sacrament. We do not come to receive this gift as those who would display a special degree of worthiness. We do not come because we have a certain pleasing act to perform in order to win God's favor. We are present at the Lord's Supper in order to be available for that which God wants to do in us and for us. It is Christ Jesus who is truly present in the bread and wine. It is He who accomplishes in these moments for the believing communicant the actual forgiveness of sins and renewal of spiritual life.

The joy which the steward finds is in part the joy of assurance that all matters are clear and settled between God and him. They are settled in that forgiveness has been received and all the wrong of the past has been blotted out. In that divine and gracious settlement the time has come for a new surrender and a new commitment of life. The joy of restoration is one of the great joys of the Christian steward. He knows that he may set forth again to do what God has called him to do.

The Christian steward, as a part of his joy in the Sacrament, finds the joy of communion with his Christian brothers. This is not an artificial and superficial experience, but is at the very heart of his participation in the Sacrament. It provides the sense of belonging to each other which comes when all the pretenses of life are laid aside. In the revealing light of the Sacrament, there is the occasion for a pledge of solid affection and mutual concern for each other. This joy of communion with fellow Christian believers and stewards will not be limited to that immediate group, however. There is the discovery in the Sacrament of the Altar of a concern for men and women beyond the Church as people who are dear to Jesus Christ and for whom Christ died. Thus, it is natural that there shall be a yearning for the redemption of mankind and an eventual communion with all men in this communion with Christ, the Savior and Lord. The joy of communion will inevitably be mixed with the desire that all men shall be saved and be restored to God.

In the Sacrament of the Altar the Christian steward is strengthened and renewed. Certainly this is a continuing need of the one who holds divine appointment and responsibility. He is strengthened because the confession of his sin and the assurance of forgiveness brings a great release to his spirit. The sanctifying and life-changing work of the Holy Spirit may proceed. The barriers are taken down. The resistance is overcome. A renewal is already taking place.

The concern which the steward naturally gives to the law of God with its requirement of being good and doing good, is surrendered at the Sacrament of the Altar. Here it is surrendered to the Gospel, to the good news of what God has done for man because He loves him. As the Christian surrenders to the Gospel and recognizes the impossibility of achieving the good life by himself, he gains a freedom from himself and from his effort to achieve. He has a fresh experience of the central truth of Christianity that "we are saved by Grace, and that not of ourselves, it is the work of God."

A part of the renewal which takes place in this extremely personal moment with Jesus Christ, is the renewal of his stewardship. Now he dares to face its implications again, for Christ has met him and refreshed and cleansed him. What he is called to be is not an impossibility. It is a use of life which can be lived out in strength because it is lived in Christ.

In I Corinthians (11:26) Paul writes: "As often as you eat this bread and drink the cup, you proclaim the Lord's death until He comes." As we explore the relation of the steward to this Sacrament, we recognize that it offers him the occasion for a Christian witness. He comes as one who is entrusted with the gospel by his act of confession and his receiving of the Body and Blood of Christ. He is proclaiming the fact that he believes in the death of Christ as the means of saving the world. This is only one way of bearing witness to his neighbors concerning this fact of the Lord's death and its meaning, but it is a very significant part of the witness.

There is, in the word which Paul records, an assurance of the final victory which is to be given to the Christian Church and to every Christian steward. Here is a note that looks forward to that final victory. This makes the celebration of the Lord's Supper a joyous and victorious occasion. It is not to be solely a looking back to tragedy, but also a looking forward to victory and to the final coming of the kingdom. The steward, in his attendance at the Lord's Supper, is clarifying for himself and for others that the Christian faith moves far ahead and lives in the very atmosphere of eternity. With this perspective he may go forth to give generously and gladly, of his life and all his means. This is the only proper and reasonable thing to do in the light of his faith in the Lord's return.

*A "guide question" to keep in mind
as you read this chapter:*

**Why do Christians give?**


## FOR GROUP DISCUSSION

Why do we so freely urge one another to use certain
abilities for the Lord—and become so hesitant to urge
one another to use the blessings of money for Him?

Since the personal element is so important in Christian
giving, why have a methodical plan for benevolence
through the congregation and the denomination?

When could a Christian steward find it proper *not* to
give?

# Chapter Ten

# Stewardship
# Emerges Into Giving

Christian stewardship carries a wide significance for living the Christian life. It has application in many areas for a responsible Christian man. These examinations of stewardship in the light of some of the main cornerstones of the Christian faith provide all the evidence needed.

It is inevitable, as was pointed out in the opening chapter, that Christian stewardship which is taken seriously finally emerges into giving. Christian stewardship cannot be separated from its implications for the use of money and the giving of money. There are a number of passages in the Gospels that tell us of our Lord's teaching about money. They throw considerable light on the fact that giving of money is involved for the Christian steward. The passages which are particularly to be noted are the following: Luke 12:16-21; Luke 16:1-13; Luke 16:19-31; Mark 10:17-22; Luke 12:32-34; Matthew 13:22; John 12:4-6. Perhaps the classic Scripture passage deals with the matter of Christian giving is that found in II Cor. 8 and 9. Here Paul addresses himself to the Corinthian Church and describes the kind of stewardship practiced by the Macedonian churches as an example to the Corinthians of the basis on which Christian giving rests. The practical instruction to con-

gregational life, which is the substance of the two letters
to the Church at Corinth, emphasizes this most significant treatment of the subject of giving.

The issues involved in the use of money, property
and the whole material world provide one of the most
critical and vulnerable areas for the Christian steward.
His specific willingness to *apply* the Christian idea, and
to undergird his confession of faith in Christ is tested.
The giving of money is certainly not the most important
obligation of the Christian, but it is one that brings
him under considerable self-examination as to the gen-
uineness of his surrender to his Lord.

It does not seem to make a great deal of difference
whether the person involved is one who has a great deal
of money and property, or one who has very little. It is
a common experience that this is just as important an
issue for the steward who knows poverty, deprivation
and hunger, as it is for the one who lives in a prosper-
ous society with its passionate emphasis on comfort, pleas-
ure, entertainment and the possession of many things. It
is a substantial issue for the Christian steward who con-
templates the possibilities of wealth and possessions inherent in the kind of technical progress familiar to this generation. The test is whether we can recognize material
wealth as something to be used, even given away, to meet
the needs of men and to serve the purposes of God, or
whether we see it as something to claim for ourselves.

Kaufman in his book *The Challenge of Christian
Stewardship*—says: "Stewardship of possessions is the effect of God's saving grace upon one's self and his property. When Jesus got Peter He also got Peter's boat.
When God gets a man with a car He gets a car to be
used in His service." (page 3)

While we bring the giving of money so emphatically

into consideration at this point, we do want to recognize that the steward's giving involves not only the giving of money. In fact, the act of giving money must never be regarded as a substitute for fulfilling other stewardship obligations.

## MOTIVES FOR GIVING

It is a common practice in civilized societies for people to give of themselves and what they have for various causes. It is also a common experience for thoughtful people to recognize that such giving is done as the result of various motives operating in people. If the insights into the true nature of stewardship, gained in these preceding chapters, are legitimate insights, then we can conclude that some motives are good and desirable, other motives fall quite short of being good.

There is the motivation which says that if a person gives he will prosper materially. It is true that in the Scripture God indicates that if people will bring their tithes and offerings He will in turn bless them. It is also clear, however, that the giving of tithes and offerings is never intended to be a mere transaction by which certain blessings are assured from God. The result may be quite different. The person who gives may not prosper at all. In fact, he may continue to find it very difficult to make ends meet. Nevertheless, he is called to be a person who gives of what he has because he is a steward of God.

There is the motive which says that we should give to equal or to excel the giving of other people. This appeal can completely shut out our relationship to God and the noble purposes for which our money can be used, and simply reflect a kind of competition of personal pride and achievement with one's neighbors. This appeal may produce money, but it is doubtful if it is a very constructive way of doing it. It may be good for our humility to learn that others in their stewardship are exceeding us. There may be a kind of a witness which we ought to hear and a self-examination which ought to take place, but it should preferably come in a different context.

It is also customary to ask people to give because it costs money to carry out benevolent enterprises. We know that these enterprises conditionally are supported by free gifts and not by taxation. We know that there are many worthy causes which would never be successfully accomplished without the free response of people who have been called upon to give of what they have. The idea, however, that we should give simply because it costs money to do certain things is not the highest motive which we would expect to find in the heart of the Christian steward. Closely related to this is the appeal to the giver to give because it costs money to run the Church, and because we receive services from the Church. This puts the whole matter on the level of a business transaction and can certainly be carried out without any particular reference to Christ, to the Creator and to the proper implications of our stewardship under God.

Sometimes the motivation calls upon our loyalty. This may be our loyalty to a person or persons. It may call upon our loyalty to the Church, particularly if the emphasis is upon the church of our fathers. It may be an appeal to our loyalty for a particular activity. Again, there are some good things which can be said about raising this kind of concern. There is a proper loyalty which we ought to have, but this is hardly the ultimate response in giving which emerges out of Christian stewardship.

Where, then, do we find our finest and best motivations? Certainly we find them when there is giving as a response to gifts God has bestowed upon us. We recognize where they have come from. We know what God wants done with them in the world, and we accept them in order to fulfill His intentions. Our giving is then an act which keeps in full view the fact of God and what he has given to us.

Another way of expressing it, which makes it more clearly Christian, is to say there is a proper stewardship of giving which is a response to God's love in Christ which climaxes in the forgiveness of sin. This motive which searches very deeply what we are and what we need produces the desire to give. No artificial or substandard motivations need to be called upon when we have come to clarity about the implications of the forgiveness of sins for our own life.

The Reverend Waldo Werning in his recent book *How to Raise Men and Money in the Church* says: "The Christian leader must be clear between the law and the gospel. Grace causes us to give; the demands of the law do not. Note these differences between grace of the New Testament and the Law of the Old Testament:

1) Law: give and live.
   Grace: live and give.
2) Law: give with a view to being something.
   Grace: makes you something with a view to give.
3) Law: saved and kept by giving.
   Grace: saved and kept unto giving.
4) Law says: "If you will give, I will bless you."
   Grace says: "I have blessed you, now give! (page 4-5).

## WHAT DO WE HAVE TO GIVE?

There are many things which we are in a position to give as the stewards of God. We can give time. This can be given to the Christian Church in its many activities and its important mission in our society. Time can be given to the congregation, to some auxiliary in the congregation, to the concerns of the larger Church organizations. Time can be given for the ministry of love to an individual or to a family. It need not go through any organized channels or forms whatsoever. There are countless opportunities which come to us in which we can take our time and surrender it to the service of God and man out of a desire to serve God and do His will. We have our intelligence and the training of that intelligence in our lives. We can use our abilities, our insights and our experience. In fact, with these gifts, as with all others, we are well advised if we do not attempt to hold them for ourselves. By their very nature and by the nature of the appointment we have from God, these are meant to be given, to be used for the good of man.

In this context, we also recognize that we have our money to give. Most of what is given, will probably be given to the Christian Church and the enterprises which are related to the Christian Church. It does not necessarily follow that *all* of it will go to the church, because we are citizens of a society in which there are many other proper and good causes to be supported for bringing benefit to mankind. These also offer an opportunity for our love and interest to reach out to other people.

A part of this money and property which we have to give will finally be left when our life is done. It

will be a part of our estate. This is also something which
we have to give. It is characteristic of the good and
thoughtful steward that he will have made his plans
for the final stewardship of money and property which
is his when life is done. He will have prepared a Christian will which will also bear witness to his Christian
faith and his love for his Redeemer. Since he is never
certain about the length of life, he prepares his will
early.

## HOW MUCH?

One of the questions which consistently arises when
stewards begin to think about giving their money away
is to ask "how much shall we give?" Sometimes this
question is a very honest and searching one. Sometimes
it is raised as a defense against too heavy a claim upon
the available resources. There is a very understandable
and helpful formula which is given to the Christian
person as he searches the Scripture. In part he will learn
this from the pages of the Old Testament, and in part
he will learn it from the New Testament.

Anyone who is acquainted with the Old Testament,
is familiar with the term "the tithe." There are certain
parts of the Christian Church which are convinced that
the rule of the tithe is to apply to every Christian person. In fact, there are churches which are very definite
and emphatic about expecting this rule for giving to be
applied in the lives of the members of their congregations. It is this writer's opinion, that while the pattern
of the Old Testament is a very important guide to the
Christian steward, it ought not be a rule which is handed
to a person as though he is under divine orders to follow it.

Dr. Kantonen very wisely says: "The tithe has assumed

far greater prominence than it has in the New Testament,
and has often been advocated on grounds quite different
from the spirit of the gospel. The Lord gave no command
concerning the tithe. We see the superficiality of the view
that tithing is the one divinely authorized and uncondi-
tionally binding method for practicing Christian stewardship. Not only does it lack a New Testament foundation,
but it lends itself to a man-centered legalism which im-
perils true religion" (p. 23). Dr. Kantonen sounds a very
important warning. When we are concerned that people
ought to be giving for the proclamation of the gospel
it is easy to go much farther than we ought to in trying
to explain to them how much they ought to give.

The one standard which Scripture does give to us
which is consistent with the spirit of the gospel is found
in Paul's letters to the Corinthians. The passage most
often quoted is I Cor. 16:2—"Give us as God has prospered." This means that God has given to each of His
stewards the responsibility for deciding what part of
his income shall be set aside for the special cause of
the gospel and the work of the Christian church. It is up
to him to come to the decision as to whether the percentage should be 10%, 12%, 15% or whatever the
proportion might be. Certainly this decision of the
steward will be made in the light of his own intelligence
and the prompting of the Holy Spirit in his own heart.
There is no abitrary proportion which is assigned to
a man because he belongs to the Christian Church. It
is to be assumed that under ordinary circumstances our
love for Christ will move us to a standard of giving
that will be at least as high as that which was called
for under the Hebrew Law. In other words, it is a
common experience to discover Christian stewards who
will be giving a portion which is equal or beyond the

tithe. The difference is that this will be their own decision arising out of the Spirit's guidance. As they search
their hearts, they search the Scripture and confront the
needs of men.

In the setting of the percentage which we will use,
it is our faith which will really establish the percentage.
We need not get into arguments with each other about
how much we are to give. We can never really settle
the issue in such a way as to bring blessing to a man if
it becomes a matter of argument. It probes into his own
relationship with Christ. Giving is not usually a question of how much money people have, but normally it is
a question of how much faith and love they have. The
call to the Christian to give is a call to the kind of faith
that dares to sacrifice, that dares to give something away
because he has an abiding conviction of the importance
of the Christian gospel.

As we ask the question "How much?" we also are led
to wonder when we ought to start in this matter of proportionate giving. Obviously, the decision is one which
ought not be postponed. We ought to decide to do it
when we are confronted with the importance of it in our
own lives. It calls for the disciplining of ourselves, which
we know we need in connection with money and with
giving. We need to hold ourselves in line. We need to
make promises to God. We need to burn our bridges
behind us in such matters. There are many well-meaning
Christian people who have intended to do something
about generous giving, but who have continually and
consistently delayed without making a definite commitment. When a commitment is made, there is hope
for that man in the accomplishing of his stewardship.
It, however, takes deliberate choice and deliberate commitment. This is the primary reason why we have dis-

covered in our Christian congregations the value of asking members to make pledges for the work of the Church.
The importance of the pledge is essentially the importance for the person who makes it. It is a matter of bringing ourselves under the choice and the discipline which
is so necessary in the face of our selfish nature.

## LEARNING HOW TO GIVE

Stewardship does not emerge into giving as a natural
result in the human heart. We need to learn how to give.
We are not born as good stewards with good habits in
such things. We give according to knowledge and faith,
not according to ability. Therefore, a sound educational
program is needed in the Christian church and all of
us as Christian stewards need to be participants in such
a learning process. All people need to be confronted
with this message, to learn the meaning of Christian
stewardship and the possible uses to which life and
means can be applied. It makes no difference whether
we are rich or poor, whether we are deeply involved
in the church or indifferent, whether we are the self-
satisfied or the spiritually hungry; we are all in need of
learning to give. We may be quite well versed in many
phases of biblical truth and be quite uninformed and
provincial in such matters as this.

Dr. Rein in his booklet "Adventures in Christian
Stewardship" gives four rules for giving. They are important to us in learning how to give.

1. Dedicate yourself with all that you are and have and
   all that you receive to God and Christ.
2. Set aside a God-pleasing portion of your income first,
   not last. Do this as often as you have an income.

3. Inform yourself about the work of your congregation and the work of your Church throughout the world and examine the causes of charity that are worthy of support; then determine intelligently how much you will give to each.

4. Bring your offering to the House of God each Sunday and make it a part of your worship.

The Christian church has learned some helpful lessons and guides for the steward who is concerned about his giving. It has learned that giving ought to be regular giving, not the kind that waits for some special stimulus or special request. We do not give primarily because there are needs to be met, but we give because God has given to us. We take a part of what He gives and apply it to the needs of which we know. Our giving should be joyous giving. It is not intended to be compulsory or to be done grudgingly. The Scripture makes plain that "God loves a cheerful giver." This certainly means any spiritual problem which causes us to hold back ought to be settled. Only then can we be in a position to accept responsibility for giving our money and all else we have or are.

It is the experience of the Church that our giving should be equitable. This means that we will intelligently take into account the kinds of needs which are to be met. We do not give everything we have to be used in our local congregation, because the Christian church in the world is much more than our congregation. We recognize the responsibilities which we have locally, but we also recognize that our responsibilities extend far out into all the world. We make equitable distribution of what we give. Along with this, we use good methods in the way we organize our giving and the manner in which we encourage other people to join us in our giving. Werning says—"God does not despise methods. Method is like packing things in a box; a good packer will get in much more than a bad one. Methods are not a necessary evil, but a necessary virtue." When we speak of methods, we have in mind such things as the annual pledge, an Every Member Visit in a congregation, the process of talking together as Christian people concerning the work of our Church, the use of weekly envelopes, of pledges, of Budgets, and all of those things which have been found to be good methods to use.

## GIVING TO AND THROUGH THE CHURCH

The Christian church, that company of Christian stewards, is called to the most vigorous affirmation of its faith in Christ which it is possible to make. In an earlier chapter reference was made to the difficulties which we have in stewardship because our understanding of the Church is so limited. It is most natural to think about the congregation to which we belong. It is much less natural to recognize our place in the family of faith which is our whole denomination, or even the family of denominations. One of the most searching examinations of Christian vision is made in studying the willingness of Christians to send money away from their home community to be joined with the gifts of others in other places. Money is not intended to be given irresponsibly, but with intelligence and a recognition of the proclamation of the gospel which ought to be accomplished in the world.

The denomination has immense value to the steward in the fulfillment of responsible stewardship. It expresses the unity of the church of Christ. It is important that this unity be expressed in the gifts and offerings which are made. The fact that we can, through our giving, express the sense of the whole Church and its mission is an asset which ought to be claimed.

"Stewardship" and "Benevolence" are words which walk arm and arm through our Christian churches, particularly those which have grown up in the American scene. In a society which has, from the beginning, called for the free gifts of people to support many good and benevolent causes, it is most natural that these two words are close comrades. It is this intimacy which has brought about those attitudes which so often assume that these words, and the ideas behind them, are synonymous.

We gather money in our churches for benevolent causes. We thus attempt to do those good things which are in keeping with our Christian faith and the commission from Christ our Lord. No such living and worthwhile endeavor will retain support from one generation to another unless the underlying principles are periodically sought out for reaffirmation and reassertion. The premises which follow are clearly behind our programs of benevolence and the continuing emphasis upon the importance of adequate support for these programs. These are the premises which call Christian stewards to give "to and through the church."

## ". . . . AND BENEVOLENCES

Perhaps the primary premise which is involved is this: *The stewardship of money, property and the whole material world emerges into the giving of them for benevolent purposes.* Here is the relationship which is so often confused. The Christian steward discovers that his stewardship ranges into many fields. One part of this is his stewardship of the material world. It is implicit in the whole message of scripture that he is to take a part of his money and give it in support of the Christian cause and the Christian message.

This assumption creates the expectation that members of our churches will give support to the benevolent causes of that church. This is not an intrusion as an unexpected part of church membership. It is seen as the eventual result for any person who is aware of his stewardship and his relationship to God and men which that steward-ship implies. It is not intended that our use of money is to be a private preoccupation, for selfish purposes, but it is intended that we give it away for intelligent and God-pleasing purposes. We are not saints because we give. We are simply keeping faith with God's intentions in making us His stewards.

The instructions which God gave to the people of Abraham concerning tithes and offerings were based on the assumption mentioned here. They were expected to give. If they did not they were guilty of misuse of what God had given them. The history of the Christian church makes clear that this relationship between stewardship of money and the giving of money for the Gospel has always been present, with some rise and fall in the tides of awareness of its implications.

A second premise in our emphasis of "benevolence" giving is: *A man's witness to his faith in the Triune God calls for such acts and such good works as are com-monly included in "benevolence."* The witness of Chris-tianity must not be divorced from the deed, whether it be the deed of courage, the deed of the builder, or the deed of love and compassion, with its remembrance of how mortal we all are and how subject to the fierce storms that can beset any single life. If the Church, or its members, surrenders the good work for others to do or leaves it undone, it has thereby surrendered one of its most important means of witnessing to Christ and to Christian truth. Among other things, it has surrendered one of its most important identifying marks.

The amount of a man's giving in proportion to his income says a very great deal about the Christian faith that he has. The decisions he makes about how to use the money he gives will bring added meaning to the witness he makes for Christ. Members of the churches ought to be regularly, patiently and imaginatively persuaded to give for benevolent purposes in order that they might join in a great and vigorous affirmation of the love of God in Christ. This is no task for which to carry apologies, but one which is worthy of our best efforts and our patient readiness to carry on in the face of those who misunderstand what is involved. To permit people in our churches to fail to make such a witness is to do injury to them, and to deny to the world what it ought to know about God and His power in human hearts.

A third premise in this series is: *"Benevolence" giving is best accomplished by the Christian steward through the Christian Church.* This is not to say that our benevolent impulses, our desire to do good because of Christ, must be limited to the Church. There is enough evidence, to be sure, that such limitations ought not to be applied. Yet, there is a great amount of evidence that when money is given in response to Christ, in affection and concern for other people, it is most wisely put to work through the Church. When the Church is supported in its work and mission we underscore the fact that we believe the solutions to the world's troubles are not political or economic and even humanitarian solutions. However valuable these may be, they are only temporary. They may arrest the forces of evil, but cannot change them.

The change worked by the Holy Spirit, in bringing men to Christ, is the lasting change.

Furthermore, the Church offers the stabilizing arm of theology to accompany our money in its mission. It is not the part of wisdom to give it solely to some agency which promises to do good deeds with it. Theology, moving arm in arm with our money, will make it accomplish its best purpose and most lasting results. It is also true that the Church is helpful in verifying our judgments of new opportunities which seem to be present, giving counsel so as to prevent mistakes in the use of what we have to give. It is possible to be very wrong because we are not well informed. Certainly the Church provides a planned and balanced program for extending and establishing the kingdom of God in men's hearts. With such a program the gifts to benevolence will receive their most varied and productive use.

A fourth premise can be stated as: *Giving for benevolences is more properly the pattern for the Christian than yielding up money for taxes to do similar work.* There is nothing sub-Christian about taxes. The support of the government is without question part of a person's stewardship. There is a commandment of God which says so. This is not a debate about taxes. The point is, however, that when the Christian confronts a decision as to whether the Church should do a certain charitable work or whether the State should do it, the assumption is that he will want the charitable work done with the benefit of Christian witness and gospel motivation. Or, when he decides to support a church-owned or church-related educational institution rather than depend only on tax-supported education, he is a partner with those who have chosen to conduct education with the Christian message directly applied.

Dr. Harry Emerson Fosdick is credited with saying: "Life is divided into two parts: The compulsory and the voluntary. They are like the sea and the land. They share the earth between them. The more there is of the one, the less there is of the other. We, therefore, have our choice: We can develop in ourselves and in our nation a strong and fruitful spiritual life that creates uncompelled character and public spirit; or, if we fail in that, coercion will come flooding in like an encroaching sea. That is the inexorable alternative." Dr. Fosdick has stated the truth which is involved in the steward's decision to give for the benevolences of the church rather than choose the way of tax-supported institutions as the only answer in our society.

A fifth premise is: *The stewardship of the Gospel calls for it to be proclaimed. The stewardship of money calls for it to be given, in Christ's name. These two implications of Christian stewardship meet when the money which is given goes to proclaim and interpret the Gospel.* Obviously, this assumption is closely related to others previously stated, but it is important enough to state separately. A Christian cannot separate himself into unrelated parts as he seeks to be faithful to God and to do God's will in the world. The treasure of what God has done for man belongs with the treasure God has given to men. We have a right to expect from the Church a call to give eagerly and generously of what we have in order to proclaim effectively the Christian message. As long as there are men to hear, in this land and in others, it is to be expected that we will supply the means to get it done . . . and supply those means without hesitance or selfish reluctance.

The last premise to be identified, although there are many others which might be included, is: *A part of responsible Christian stewardship is the gift which sustains the Christian agencies of learning, the gift which strengthens the health and welfare institutions of the Church, and the gift which upholds and encourages those at the frontier posts of the Church.* The support of the benevolence program of the Church is a significant process of bringing the reinforcements of money and confidence to undergird those institutions through which the Church is to accomplish a large part of its mission in a society. We are stewards of these institutions. We are entrusted with the Church and its outposts, whether they are on this continent or on another.

In accepting this trust we unite our voices with those of our fathers in the Church. We retain the foundations of the past and move to new achievements without retracing too many steps and going back to re-learn what others have learned before us. We do well as the stewards of God to become a part of the responsibilities inherent in the church from generation to generation. Our participation in the benevolences of the church is one way of revealing that we are mature and responsible people in the Church's present and continuing witness.

Yes, stewardship emerges into giving, and our giving is an important Christian exercise and witness. It can be accomplished primarily through the church, with intelligence, earnestness and thankfulness. For this we are called by God. It is this which we hold in our hands.

# Bibliography

1. A Theology For Christian Stewardship, by T. A. Kantonen. Muhlenberg Press.
2. I Believe in the Holy Spirit, by Fredrik Wisloff. Augsburg Publishing House.
3. Living the Ten Commandments, by Carroll E. Simcox. Morehouse-Gorham Co.
4. Living The Creed, by Carroll E. Simcox. Morehouse-Gorham Co.
5. Living The Lord's Prayer, by Carroll E. Simcox. Morehouse-Gorham Co.
6. The Kingdom of God, by John Bright. Abingdon-Cokesbury Press.
7. The Cost of Discipleship, by Dietrich Bonhoeffer. The Macmillan Co.
8. Life Together, by Dietrich Bonhoeffer. Harper and Bros.
9. Doing the Truth, by James A. Pike. Doubleday Press.
10. Senior Confirmation Book, Jacob Tanner. Augsburg Publishing House.
11. Christian Giving, by V. S. Azariah. World Christian Books.
12. The Message of Stewardship, by Ralph Cushman. Abingdon-Cokesbury.
13. What Are You Worth, by G. Curtis Jones. The Bethany Press.
14. Teaching Christian Stewardship, by Glenn McRae. The Bethany Press.
15. Adventures in Christian Stewardship, by R. C. Rein, Concordia Publishing House.
16. Ten Studies in the Stewardship of the Christian Man, by Mars Dale, Augsburg Publishing House.
17. Twelve Baskets Full, by Margaret T. Applegarth. Harper and Brothers.
18. The Use of Life, by Frederick Ward Kates. Harper and Bros.
19. How to Raise Men and Money in the Church, by Waldo Werning. American Lutheran Publicity Bureau.
20. Full-Grown in Christ, by A. M. Kraabel. Augsburg Publishing House.